GLASS
for a beautiful home

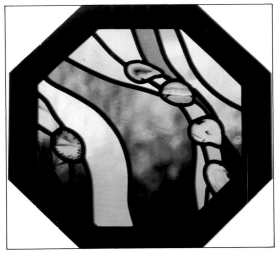

GLASS

BEAUTIFUL HOME SERIES

First edition for the United States and Canada published 1990 by Barron's Educational Series, Inc.

© Copyright 1988 by Merehurst Limited
By arrangement with Dunestyle Publishing Ltd.

First published in Great Britain in 1988 by
Merehurst Limited, London, England.

All inquiries should be addressed to:
Barron's Educational Series, Inc.
250 Wireless Boulevard
Hauppauge, New York 11788

Library of Congress Catalog Card No. 90-17
International Standard Book No. 0-8120-6172-1

Library of Congress Cataloging-in-Publication Data
Lloyd, Matthew.
   Glass for a beautiful home. Matthew Lloyd & Janet
      Blackmore. 160p. (Beautiful home series)
First published in Great Britain in 1988 by
Merehurst Limited, London, England — T.p. verso.
   ISBN 0-8120-6172-1
   1. Glass painting and staining, 2. Decoration and
ornament, Architectural. I, Blackmore, Janet,
II, Title, III, Series, NK5304, LBB 1990
748.5 –dc20   90-17 CIP

Printed in Italy by New Interlitho s.p.a., Milan

0123   987654321

Half title page A modern stained glass picture which looks really effective when suspended in a window. *Prismo Stained Glass*
Title page A scenic design works well when continued across the panels of this stripped pine entrance door. *Matthew Lloyd*
Contents page This large circular window, with a stylized flower design, would make a splendid feature to any room — adding light while obscuring the unattractive view beyond. *Celtic Glass*

GLASS
for a beautiful home

Matthew Lloyd & Janet Blackmore

Matthew Lloyd & Janet Blackmore

BARRON'S

NEW YORK · TORONTO

CONTENTS

Right A restrained geometric grid supports subtle details of formal pictorial images mixed with a floral centerpiece, in this domed window set into a high paneled ceiling.

Above A library and office — converted from a chapel attached to a manor house — lit by a modern window displaying family symbolism of the owners.

The effects of light falling through colored glass have always been a source of fascination. Natural light gleams through stained glass, creating a seasonal kaleidoscope of lovely color mutations; electricity is transformed into a romantic glow. Glass is the only decorative device that allows this element of subtle change and unpredictability and it is this variable quality that makes stained glass such a profoundly creative medium.

Yet, many architects and designers, when confronted by the fascinating caprice of glass, are confused and dismissive. A Victorian critic expressed these doubts perfectly when, after contemplating a stained glass window, he exclaimed "To my mind, the opalescent flummydiddle was exceedingly pretty and, at the same time, a blasphemy against all artistic standards." Too many conventional designers have rigid ideas as to "artistic standards" and this adherence to the "rules" of art has prevented them from recognizing that colored glass is an art form that appeals to the feelings not the intellect and that because colored light evokes a strong emotional response, it is an art form ideally suited to both religious and domestic architecture.

The massive Gothic cathedrals of Europe, such as Chartres in France, were enhanced by great, glimmering stained glass windows that threw rainbow light down into deep, dim interiors and inspired awe amongst medieval worshippers. In the Middle East, architects delighted in colored glass and mosaic work. The mosques of the Arab world shimmer with sensuous, sparkling light, expressing the poetry and passion of Islamic culture.

Domestic architecture, and the decorative motifs of a home, ought to demonstrate the intimate, emotional life of the people who inhabit that house. Glass allows wonderfully varied and individual

Below The elegantly proportioned panels in this small Victorian bathroom are emphasized by the use of strong perpendicular line.

Right Frosted glass, with a view of smudged external scenes, forms an interesting white-light background to the dense graphic foliage of the stained glass plant form.

expression, yet the concept of stained glass in our homes seems such an innovative idea that architects rarely consider including colored glass in their designs for houses and apartment buildings.

The Glass Dream

In the first half of our century, architects were enormously excited by the use of glass. Avant garde architects dreamed of glass houses, glass domes; they waxed lyrical and talked of "glass dreams." A German writer, Paul Scheerbart, produced a slim but influential book called *Glasarchitecture*, which was published in 1914. He described his vision of glass building as a "paradise on earth" and wrote of "double walls of colored glass" with lighting fitted between these walls, and even his furniture was to be made of glass supported by brightly enameled steel legs. He moved beyond the glass house to a glass metropolis of amazing jewel-like buildings. His volume appeared in the same year as the famous Werkbunde Exhibition in Cologne that introduced and promoted the glass dreams of contemporary architects, particularly the model factory by Gropius and the glass dome by Taut.

Some marvelous glass buildings emerged from this era such as the Seagram Building designed by Mies van der Rohe and Philip Johnson in 1954, and Lever House in 1952, the architect of which was Gordon Bunshaft of Skidmore, Owings and Merrill. Obviously, glass buildings are not yet a practicality for domestic architecture, but we can make a space for our own glass paradise within our homes.

While Paul Scheerbart and his ilk dreamt of entire cities built of glass, there were more realistic architects who used colored glass as a live component of architecture, who made philosophical analyses of the effects of stained glass, and who developed a profound understanding of the life-enhancing quality

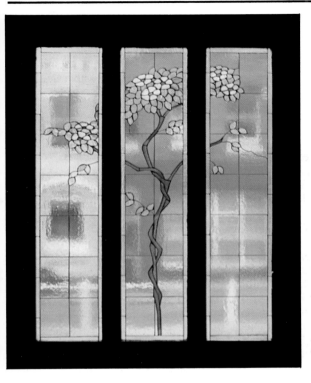

Below This porthole window shows how stained glass can be used effectively in small areas. The flower theme has been taken from the pattern present on the tiles.

of colored light. They described glass in terms of "transparent membranes" or "colored membranes", thus recognizing the material as a fundamental element in the skin of a building. Certain concepts of light, color, and function emerged from their work, and should be considered when making the most gracious use of stained glass as a decorative element in the home.

Glass Aspects

Architects have learned to maintain a delicate balance between colored light and airy space. "Strong, bright colors and complex designs can overpower a room or prevent a person from visually escaping to the outdoors and stained glass should be used with an unpretentious simplicity that expands the space and does not oppress."

There are occasions when the white glare of light through glass needs to be tempered, and stained glass solves the problem of windows that are necessary for allowing light to enter the room, yet a decorative window can delineate spaces of colored and white light, creating an effect that softens the glare and, at the same time allows an adequate supply of natural light. The dull view, now incorporated into the window design, becomes an interesting decorative element.

Plain glass is often used from habit or convention when stained glass would be the superior choice. As far back as 1876, one American writer on the decorative arts, Donald Mitchell, pointed out that colored glass was "full of suggestion to those living in cities whose rear windows look upon neglected or dingy courts, where the equipment of a window with rich designs would be a perpetual delight."

It is not unusual, in contemporary apartments, to find kitchens (and bathrooms) designed into small corners with tiny windows opening on to a view of a brick wall or the plumbing pipes. Such rooms can be elevated from the ordinary, even the dingy, into a warm, multidimensional space through the introduction of windows of glowing color.

Below These porthole windows provide splashes of color in the plain brick wall that relect in the water of the pool.

Even when the light, or the view, are not primary considerations, stained glass serves as a purely decorative device, to be used to great effect. Fanlights on doors, or window transoms, become delightful, rich jewel-like images adding subtle, changing color and pleasing detail to the style of a room. Even a pale or inadequate light supply will combine with the colored glass to create a vibrant tonality that is lacking in paint or textiles.

For this is the fascination of stained glass that through the shifting, changing effect of colored light, the moods and nuances of space are continually articulated and reiterated. Perhaps this element is best demonstrated in the transformation wrought by a stained glass screen. The function of a screen is to divide and block off space, but constructed of stained glass, this screen will extend the structure of a room by the conversion of light, an effect impossible to achieve with any other material.

Light Tones

Color is the powerful, primary consideration in the design and use of stained glass. A thoughtful understanding of the space where the light is going to fall is required and an honest appraisal of the significance of color must be made. There are colors that dominate and absorb space, colors that soothe or excite, that are serene or dynamic. Colors will affect the ambience of a home, and are an unavoidable statement of the emotional balance of that home.

Although the colors of stained glass are uninhibited and enriched by light, the glazier's craft must fit a tighter discipline than that of the painter. The glazier must work within the lead strips (called cames) that are an essential part of stained glass in that they support the material. However, these strips are not tolerated as simply an essential structural requirement, but must be considered as an integral aspect of the design. Medieval glass craftsmen achieved an effect close to mosaic work in their manner of closely holding the glass within a fretwork of lead, and their style is quite different from that of the great modern window designer, Johannes Schreiter of Germany. His lead strips stretch and curve in free graphic lines that seem to be drawn across the glass sections, rather than supporting them. Brian Clarke in Britain also uses his lead strips to "draw" his designs of glass.

Glass Essentials

Stained glass enjoyed a wild vogue in the late Victorian and the Edwardian era, but fell into unfashionable decline in the mid-twentieth century. Modern architecture is slowly taking cognizance of the desirable qualities of colored glass, but generally these are ignored in our cities that are increasingly a conglomeration of drab mass-designed dwelling places. Technological civilization offers easily

Left These two panels are designed in the style of Frank Lloyd Wright, whose sense of balance, rhythm, and proportion were his trademark.

available mass-production of every commodity we require — or even don't require. The need to make an individual statement grows more and more imperative, and there is one area where self-expression can be fully realized. That is in our homes. Each single unit of a million mass-designed homes can be given its own peculiar identity, and be lifted beyond the dull repetition of its neighbors.

In our domestic lives, there is space to develop a personal motif, and a unique window design, an extraordinary doorway or a romantic rainbow of light in the bathroom are our private announcements of paradise.

Above This small arched window, one of a pair placed on either side of a chimney breast, reflects the occupation of the owner. The windows each have their own color and the notes are made of glass globes.

CHAPTER 1

Left and right Slumped glass and slabs of Brazilian agate were used to create these magnificent designs for the entrance hall of a house in Florida.

Traditionally, and logically, windows are the great "canvas" of glass art. As the primary source of light, windows are intrinsically the focal point of a room, and the urge to play with that light is irresistible. The thin, airy surface of the glass, breaking the mass of impenetrable wall, invites design and decoration.

The architects of medieval churches sought many ways to interrupt the huge masonry of their buildings. With fantasies of filigree stonework and elegant traceries of pattern breaking the lintel over a door, or with soaring arches, statues, and gargoyles, they created lyrical movement within the massive shell of walls. But the windows provided the obvious, the natural contrast to these walls, a contrast that could be emphasized with decorated, colored glass.

A high level of artistic achievement was attained by the glass craftsmen of medieval Europe. Although their technological range was limited, they achieved rich and dynamic colors in their stained glass. As these windows were dedicated to the glory of God, the craftsmen depicted biblical stories and characters, and incorporated into these images, decorations that repeated the motifs of the illuminated manuscripts produced by medieval priests. Plants, animals, and geometric shapes delighted the medieval artist.

Historians claim that the craftsmen designed these religious scenes for illiterate worshippers who needed pictures to explain the biblical message, but these strange and wonderful glass stories were not the primary purpose of these stained glass windows. The craftsmen designed, in accordance with the ethos of their time, religious tales and symbols, but who could see these pictures, placed as they were, way up in the soaring heights of the Romanesque cathedral? No, the true significance of these stained

Right White light combines with color and gives beautiful tones to the granite texture of these bathroom walls.

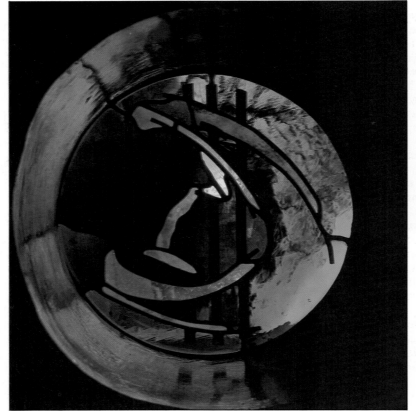

Above Sweeping color blended into darker tones is a design solution that enhances, without emphasis, the circle of the window.

Right Outside the bathroom window relies on a purely decorative surface that has its own integrity without the effect of light.

glass windows is found in the magical colored light that transformed the severity of the deep interiors.

The stained glass of the medieval glazier is known as "pot-metal." Color was created by fusing the glass and the dyeing agent, generally a metallic oxide, together in the melting pot. This was done to all glass except ruby glass, which was so dark that it was coated on one side with clear glass. Designs were then formed by grinding the ruby until clear glass showed through.

However, these old medieval techniques fell into neglect, as religious and political upheavals overtook Europe. The Reformation and consequent separation of the Christian church meant the decline of the old attachment between craftsmen and church. A stern reaction to the luxurious beauty of the Catholic church overcame the new churchmen and opulent decoration was discouraged. The art of stained glass became a rare skill, the craftsmen dispersed, the technology forgotten. The technique of painting enamels onto the glass gradually overtook the old system, and painters replaced the glass artists. This practice became widespread during the seventeenth century when pot-metal glass became scarce, although light does not penetrate paint with the same facility as it glows through colored glass.

The Arts and Crafts Revival

During the Industrial Revolution of the nineteenth century, artists began again to show interest in the techniques of stained glass. As the ancient rural pattern of life was disrupted by machinery that replaced the labor of man, and that created urban sprawls where once had been fields and villages, so a wave of nostalgia gripped artists and intellectuals. Saddened by the disappearance of the old handicrafts, these men wished to retain the slower, more serene methods of work, and

Above This door combines color and white light with the use of gentle stained glass tones surrounding a diamond of clear glass.

Above A tightly-packed leaf design recalls William Morris but asymmetrical sky shapes reveal a modern development.

they sought to revive pre-machine methods of production.

A romantic view of a golden medieval era prompted research into the manners and architecture of the Middle Ages. Nostalgia led to a renewed interest in embroidery, weaving, carving, and stained glass. In France, Viollet le Duc studied and renovated the Romanesque churches of his native land. He wrote about his obsession and his research into techniques of medieval stained glass. In England, the nostalgia was strongly felt, and the English Gothic Revival had a powerful influence all over Europe and the United States.

The leading artist to emerge from this English movement was William Morris. He wished to recreate the medieval guild system where artisans and artists worked closely together producing beautiful handmade objects. He loathed the factory system, and the mass-produced goods it spawned. His ideas formed the basis of the Arts and Crafts Movement and his artistic preferences were for the intricate "natural" motifs of Celtic and Romanesque work. Morris created splendid stained glass work, but his interest lay primarily in the rich pattern and color of the medievalists.

In the manifesto for his own decorating company, Morris mentions "Stained Glass, especially with reference to its harmony with Mural Decoration." The skill required in stained glass did not interest him unduly. Morris and his colleague Burne-Jones were happy to paint on glass if that gave them the right decorative effect. Although Morris investigated the technology, he was not absorbed by it. The glaziers who experimented endlessly with stained glass were the American craftsmen.

Below This set of French windows is unusual in that the original design depicts a pair of wild fowl taking off from a marsh and includes the use of painted, etched, and flashed glass. The birds are cut from handblown glass that has been expertly painted and stained to create lifelike detail. The reeds and water have also been painted and closely resemble nature. The leadwork however is less appealing because it has been used purely as a method of construction. No effort has been made to make the shapes of glass mimic the design content. However, in this instance, it is of less importance because of the strength of the design.

Right The view is not hidden but enhanced by translucent glasses in a design harmonious to the landscape.

The American Heritage

A great glass industry developed in the United States for a number of reasons. Americans were not inhibited by a tradition of religious expression in stained glass, and neither were they averse to using machinery and technology in advancing their craft. They were excited by the Industrial Revolution rather than repulsed. An extremely wealthy class of merchants and industrialists grew from the industrial upsurge in America. This class was not restrained, housed, or furnished by aristocratic family possessions. They created their own wealth, and they spent it on lavish homes and office buildings. The glaziers of America persuaded them to use stained glass in both types of architecture and "an ancient art was steadily transformed by American materials, styles and techniques."

It is the tragedy of art glass that it is comparatively fragile, and that it has for so long been dismissed as a "minor art." The problematical discipline of the form has allowed stained glass to be perceived as a "craft," and so its beauty and the achievement of its practitioners have long been neglected. But, in nineteenth-century America, stained glass reached a remarkable popularity and expertise.

In the latter half of the century, two men in New York experimented endlessly to achieve the glowing beauty of Romanesque glass, and to move their technique beyond even that great era of stained glass. They were John La Farge and Louis Comfort Tiffany. The latter artist said; "I could not make an imposing window with paint" and his stained glass is remarkable for its color, for its texture, and for its technology.

In 1881 both Tiffany and La Farge were recognized by the prestigious *Scribner's Monthly* for their contribution to art glass. The magazine felt that these two men had introduced a new glass

Left Floral forms are suited to the art of stained glass. The curved lines and shapes translate easily to the medium.

Below left Art Nouveau with its use of sinuous lines and pure color is always popular in art glass.

Below The tendrils and elegant leaf shapes create an effect of movement against a geometric grid.

Left This ceiling of stained glass
reflects the best of American Art
Glass design in its ornate precision.

Below This small panel relies on an
airy and delicate use of cames for
pure graphic impact.

industry to the United States, and wrote that
because of their work "new styles of opalescent
glass, new methods of mixing colours in the
glasshouse have been tried and with many surprising
and beautiful results."

John La Farge did not possess the same business
acumen as Tiffany, and his work never achieved the
same popularity. Louis Comfort Tiffany and his
Tiffany Studios designed and installed hundreds of
stained glass windows which could be seen in half
the United States and in such illustrious institutions
as the Smithsonian, Yale University, and the White
House.

Louis Comfort Tiffany

The name of Tiffany has "become synonymous
with American stained glass" and he "carved his
reputation as the premier nineteenth century
American stained glass artist who approached the
medium with other than medieval instincts."

Louis Comfort Tiffany was an extraordinary
combination of artist and entrepreneur. His artistic
skill was of great taste and distinction, and he was
thrilled by the economic and industrial power of his
country. His was not an exclusive, elitist nature that
elevated "Art" to an esoteric realm, and he saw
industrialization as a means to fairer distribution.
"Already," he once said with satisfaction, "legislative
halls, railway stations and opera houses are liable to
be more beautiful than the palaces of the rich."

He started his career as a painter, and was
immediately successful. The power of his work lay
in his talent as a colorist, and it is this talent
that elevates his art glass above that of his contem-
poraries. He did not long confine his creative energy
to painting but soon moved into interior design and
began his first experiments in stained glass.

Above Opaque and antique streaky glass has been used to create mountain scenes. This window in Colorado expresses a love of the Southwestern American landscape.

At this stage, around 1880, Tiffany and La Farge worked at the same glass house, but the two men were competitive and did not work together long. Later, Tiffany had his own glass house in Corona, Queens, where he had 300 tons of glass that were classified into some 500 colors and varieties.

Tiffany longed to reproduce a painterly effect in stained glass without the use of paint. "Glass covered with brushwork produces an effect both dull and artificial," he cried. He translated his richly imaginative vision with such artistic skill that his work continues to please and influence a modern audience. His technical virtuosity is compelling. "The stippling of a bird's feather, the roughness of bark, the gleam of water, all are reproduced in the great pictorial windows he created, but none of these textures is drawn or marked on the glass." The pieces of glass are a collage of colors, colors striped, mottled, patterned, and spotted; these color variations were themselves in the glass. He would match all the pieces into the design so that colors and textures flowed in a painterly manner. The absence of brushwork allowed the light to pass unhindered through the glass.

Landscapes and plant studies were subjects favored by Tiffany himself, but he often executed commissions that demanded heroic or biblical figures. He designed stained glass for the American Red Cross headquarters in Washington, D.C. and used a fantasy theme of the Age of Chivalry, with handsome, bold knights and brave, sweet women to illustrate this theme. He portrayed biblical figures of gentle gravity when designing a memorial to the Confederate dead for Old Blandford Church, Pittsburgh, Virginia. But even in these commissions, Tiffany found ways of introducing plants and flowers.

One of his most lyrical works was a portrayal of

Left The effect of colored glass fully exploits reflections and ripples of water, as in this peaceful rural scene. It is a medium well suited to represent movement of light and shade.

The challenge of representing large landscapes has excited glaziers for generations. This window in a house in Florida depicts the changing seasons and is a superb example of this genre.

"The Four Seasons." Here, the pictorial descriptions of each season were set in a medallion effect, surrounded by a decorative border of lyrical shapes and brilliant color.

Tiffany's obsession with light and color led him into purely abstract designs, but these pieces he preferred to keep for display in his own home.

In his glass experiments he "produced irregularities of surface to vary and enhance the qualities of light transmission," and he experimented ceaselessly with color. He was dissatisfied with the thin color being produced by most commercial firms. He wanted the thick, dense colors of rubies and emeralds, or an indigo blue, he wanted mother-of-pearl and glimmering black.

Tiffany's contribution to the "ancient art" is a grand gesture of daring inventiveness, a vivid imagination, and a bold use of technology. He was a great experimental artist who lifted stained glass from its traditional religious mystique and promoted it as a popular, egalitarian art form.

Art Glass

H.Weber Wilson in his extensive study of *Great Glass in American Architecture* has said that "by utilizing a veritable rainbow of sensuously textured glasses, emphasizing complex, tightly leaded compositions, and incorporating a luscious assortment of jewels and other special inserts, American glass artists fashioned ornamental configurations and naturalistic scenes with profound brilliance and realism."

Stained glass was incorporated into architecture, so that the entire facade of a building became a closely-linked surface pattern of brick and ornamental window. Some of these facades still stand, a mute testimony to the essential harmony between architect and glazier. Windows were

Right Flower motifs are ideal for domestic use. They are familiar and comforting images in the home. This circular form is both elegant and reassuring.

Below Another, more stylized, landscape is used in this stripped pine entrance door.

turned into distinctive areas of pictorial and decorative interest with some glaziers, in imitation of Tiffany, achieving an almost painterly effect in their combinations of color and texture. Light remained, of course, an integral element in the composition, and light was bent, caught and contained. These glass artists would fit "jewels" into the pattern, thick chunks of glass manufactured to resemble jewels, and these would catch the light causing it to sparkle and refract. Some used beveled glass to create glittering lines on the edges of flat color, others used "bulls-eyes," heavy, uneven circular sections to alter the quality and density of light. Many of these techniques were developed from the technical advances in glassmaking and coloring produced by Louis Comfort Tiffany and John La Farge.

Tiffany's luscious but representational landscapes, and his decorative borders also influenced many glaziers. Richly colored scenic windows became available to middle America from the pattern books of commercial glaziers. These were often charming domestic studies, of cozy hills and little cottages, well suited to the decoration of a modest home. There was another influence affecting the design preferences of Americans, and this came from the American Arts and Crafts Movement.

Obviously, this sprang directly from the ideals of William Morris, and was a stylistic movement dedicated to craftsmanship. However, the English preference for an ornate, romantic aesthetic, its mixture of new Gothic and Art Nouveau, did not sit easily with the American disciples. They chose a native style of cleaner, simpler lines known as the "Mission" or "Shaker" style. This native idiom was a direct statement from a pioneer heritage in which furniture was built in basic functional proportions, as were homes and decorations. Glaziers interpreted

Below Mirrors are an excellent way of increasing the effect of stained glass.

the "Mission" style into glass designs of graphic simplicity, reducing plant forms into their basic components without the fanciful line of Art Nouveau.

But the Arts and Crafts Movement did leave a profound mark for "this interest in crafts and craft work has continued right into the present time, and is undoubtedly a key factor in the long-standing secular support of American residential stained glass art."

The glass artists considered carefully not only the effects of the light falling into a room through their stained glass designs, but they wished also to create a decorative delight so that a passerby, not seeing the light effects, would find pleasure in the color and composition of the window. The new techniques in glassmaking, and the bold, secular use of stained glass, allowed for exciting developments of the art in the nineteenth century, yet, in a sense, it was this obsession with decorative windows and the excitement of producing a wide range of richly-colored glass that finally exhausted the art. The fantasized motifs of Art Nouveau began to appear with more and more frequency in the American art glass world. This apparently complex and convoluted style is actually easy to translate into stained glass designs. The strongly curved flat forms, with simplified floral motifs, and a free expression of color, allowed glass studios to construct many frames quickly and cheaply. Although not a popular style in other American art forms, such as architecture, Art Nouveau soon dominated stained glass products, with little that was original or powerful in its statement. This pervasive fashion in stained glass ultimately made a mockery of both the glazier's skill and the individual craftsman's longing for a handcrafted statement.

The glazier's early originality degenerated into a

Below The vibrant design for a bathroom window was taken from a design on an ancient vase that translated successfully into glass. The two figures completely fill the composition and, in the background, the sky is red with flame and heavy with smoke.

routine production of complicated pictorial effects designed in heavy fruity colors, and the market was flooded with patterned windows from numerous factories. Stained glass began to overwhelm, rather than enhance, architectural interiors.

Architecture itself grew heavily ornamental; neo-Gothic turrets and towers, or Art Nouveau fantasies dominated fashionable taste until World War I. After this catastrophic upheaval, artists dismissed the giddy and extravagant style of the Edwardian world, and looked for a sterner, more sober, idiom. They determined to create a modern style that combined the functional with the abstract.

The ornamental richness of stained glass windows was scorned; glass was kept "pure" or used as a building material, not as a decoration. It was only after World War II that the "ancient art" was

Left This front door is designed in the style of Rousseau and depicts a single scene. The design is made up of three windows linked by a tree whose trunk and branches serve to hold the picture together. The strong use of vibrant colors, gives the work a richness one would expect to find in the real jungle.

Below Stained glass allows a wide variety of textures. Two landscapes are combined in this design — an arid desert scene and a mysterious range of mountains.

revived and extended to even further expression.

The Modern Glaziers

In this, the latter half of the twentieth century "stained glass has been restored as a monumental art occupying a significant position within its architectural setting." Glass artists have a vigorous, experimental approach to their craft, and make full use of all the options offered by the technology of our times.

Modern stained glass is enriched and nourished by other disciplines, drawing for inspiration on painting, sculpture, and architecture. Some of the most superb glass artists are also painters, and find no loss of status in having their work translated into glass by a master glazier. The British stained glass artist, John Piper, has worked closely with Patrick Reyntiens, a craftsman who interprets Piper's paintings into glass. (Louis Comfort Tiffany was considered radical because he translated the work of Toulouse-Lautrec, Pierre Bonnard, and others into stained glass.)

The development of modern art has provoked considerable advances in stained glass design. The principles of abstract art can be translated perfectly into stained glass. In fact, stained glass is the perfect expression of these principles, offering as it does, the opportunity to express pure, flat color, held within a confining line, but subtly shifting its symbolism with changing light tones.

Architects also, in the drab postwar years in Europe, slowly began to appreciate the use of color in buildings. "Contemporary achievements in structural engineering allow for the maximum use of glass" and as glass is used ever more frequently to construct entire walls, so architects have been forced to concentrate upon the effects of light. Inevitably, this has drawn them into the age-old

Below This is a free standing framed panel based on a Bauhaus design, made for a home in New Orleans.

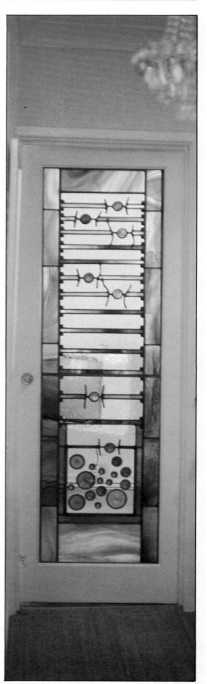

Right The shimmering and romantic effects of streaky glass are controlled by panels of clear light in this door.

fascination with light falling through colored glass. Stained glass yet again has become an important element in architectural design, despite a continued resistance from conservative designers, who remain chary of "the unpredictability of colored glass."

The most exciting developments in modern stained glass have been in Germany. The reconstruction program that followed the war gave that country an opportunity to build extensively and experimentally. This program gave a high priority to religious needs and many new churches were built. Once again, the glass artist found his craft in demand, especially as the appreciation for monumental stained glass grew from its use in ecclesiastic buildings and spread into secular architecture.

Frank Lloyd Wright

Many inspired glass artists emerged from reconstructed Germany, among them Ludwig Schaffrath and Johannes Schreiter whose powerful abstract glass walls and windows have influenced all modern stained glass artists. But even these men were nourished by the American achievements of the last century. The Chicagoan architect Frank Lloyd Wright was the finest mentor. He anticipated the abstract art of the twentieth century in his stained glass "Prairie" style windows, and he understood the symbiotic relationship of architecture and stained glass. Many of his architectural plans automatically included specifications for stained glass as an integral part of his building. His chief design contribution in stained glass craft was in the concept of decorative windows used as screens or *grilles*. He allowed clear glass to be incorporated within the design of colored glass, and he set the glass in zinc strips or cames. The strength of these cames eliminates the need for horizontal support bars, which would spoil the visual effects in the clear glass sections. Wright favored a

FLAT SURFACES

Right Internal doors constructed of glass give light and decorative value to the room.

Below In this glass screen the cames make a graphic statement that belies their supportive function.

Below This framed fixed panel has a design based on the theme of water. Light and line are used to form an abstract concept.

vertical line in his stained glass, and developed a very personal idiom in his elongated, stylized plant forms.

Modern glass artists use this *grilles* concept with great freedom of interpretation. In the windows for the Chapel, St. Antonius Hospital, Eschweiler in West Germany, Ludwig Schaffrath has used white glass delineated with significant and original came work.

In a brilliant and haunting stained glass wall of variegated blues and aquamarines Johannes Schreiter has framed the whole in sections of white light, and then he has "dribbled" a line of white here and there down his dense blue drama. This was designed for the chapel of the Exerzitienhaus Johannesbund, Leutsdorf/Rhein.

Other eccentric interpretations of Wright's simple *grilles* concept are made by Hochem Peonsgen, also of Germany.

The Personal Glazier

It is ironical that industrial and technological advances have brought us closer to the pleasures of handcrafted production, for these advances were the very things that the Arts and Crafts Movement feared would kill craft individualism forever. We share, with William Morris, a yearning for human expression and achievement, and a healthy suspicion for the mass-produced; but, unlike those earnest Victorians, we exploit the opportunities technology has brought us.

Glass technology has brought glass craft into our personal sphere of activity. Because of it, we can be our own glaziers, our own glass artist, and practice the extraordinary craft of transforming light through our own stained glass designs. But the art of the glazier remains a fierce discipline and the difficulties of creation mean that the end result must

Right This front door introduces vitality but retains maximum light effect in a dark Victorian entrance.

Below Strong dashes of color contrive to pattern the inner wall.

be fully anticipated to avoid the disappointment of ill-thought creativity.

Glass art is not the same as painting or sculpture, even though these may have their influence. Unlike these arts, glass has an element that is eccentric and unpredictable, ultimately beyond the control of the artist. Paint or marble can be mastered, but light cannot be. No matter how wonderful the choice of glass, or how superb the tools available, the work of the stained glass craftsman is useless without his own essential sensitivity to light.

Before conceiving any design in stained glass, concentrate on the effects of light. Observe the phenomena as you leave your front door, how light alters as it reflects off the texture of walls or is lost in the smooth bright surface of an automobile. Watch how the sky changes as the sun moves across the

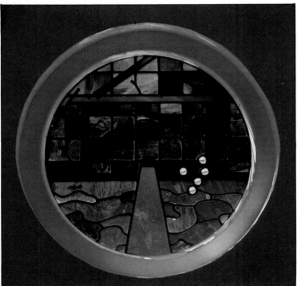

Above Left These windows were commissioned to create harmony with a fifteenth century building.

Below left This modern art glass is a masterly example of light effects in an intricate design concept.

day, for even a dull sun has an interesting quality of light. The most important light for you is the one that falls through your window, think carefully about that light. John Piper, in his stained glass for Canterbury Cathedral, constructed his color so that the brightest light was gathered into the center of the grand design. Where and how do you want light to fall?

This deliberate struggle towards an awareness of light will bring gratifying confidence. You will find that your new perceptions will enrich your design decisions as you work upon stained glass.

Which Window

Colored light will alter the environment. When designing your window, it is important to assess which environment is to be modified. Will your window be part of a narrow hall, or is it in the main living room? How much natural light is required in that area?

Usually, a window in the living room is a vital source of light, and it may not be wise to plan a full color window for this room. In an entrance hall, the fall of colored light may create a warm, welcoming atmosphere in an otherwise dull area. Or if this entrance is a large but ordinary space, the stained glass window can make a dramatic statement.

There are rooms in the home that are by nature intimate and cozy. One is the kitchen, where the equipment and fittings are functional but the purpose, to feed and nourish the family, creates an atmosphere of affectionate well-being. Here a stained glass window designed with a personal statement, a family motif, becomes an important affirmation of the kitchen atmosphere.

The bathroom, too, is a utility room where the bath, the basin, the plumbing are clinically functional, yet it is a place of fantasy, perfume, and

Below The bathroom is ensuite to the master bedroom and, when illuminated from the bathroom, the panel glows meditatively into the bedroom.

Below right Beyond these windows is a double glazed unit, totally out of keeping with the Victorian style of the bathroom. The panels were introduced to add to the style of the room and hide the double glazing.

privacy. The decorative effect of stained glass enhances this ambience, and emphasizes the luxurious use of the bathroom. And, in a different mood, the living room, a more public area, can carry an abstract pattern that makes a beautiful but discreet statement of the private life within.

Because your stained glass will be an important decorative element, give the design careful analysis.

A study of the great master glass artists introduces a wide variety of design styles to the hobbyist. A wander through history inspires unusual, or little-used concepts, which can add to the pleasure of creating your own style.

Medieval church windows, although limited in use of color, offer marvelous details of animals or complex geometric combinations. Tiffany windows vary enormously from grand pictorial scenes to lyrical, flowing floral essays. The controlled beauty of a William Morris or Burne-Jones window uses a mixture of austere, simplified plant motifs and romantically-executed figures.

The modern German glazier William Buschulte relies on an unusually strong emphasis in the complicated patterning of the cames (the lead work) while Ludwig Schaffrath develops sweeping curves of color. A graphic use of cames and color can be seen in the work of Brian Clarke in England.

Armed by familiarity with great works, the home glass artist will find the confidence to express his own choice in designs.

Design Discipline

Glass art is formalized and limited by the very nature of glass and its own fragile limitations, but any study of the designs used in nineteenth-century United States will reassure the enthusiast. The rich experimental work of that period reveals that a

Right Before the curtains and stained glass were produced, this window was a real problem area. The large square format completely dominated the landing stair and hallway of this house. The curtains soften the shape and add dimension to the glass.

satisfying range of shapes can be cut and fashioned in glass. Before drawing your own personal design, do observe what controls and disciplines are demanded by the material.

Glass art does not allow spontaneous inspiration. It is an art that is also a craft, and so tools, techniques, and material must be used with a sustained discipline, that combines control and pre-planned designing. The style of Art Nouveau is ideally suited to glass art. It is a style that favors flat color more than shaded, painterly tones, and prefers a clear line to separate shape from color. The artists of this style "arranged nature according to their vision, giving stems and leaves regular undulations, always with an eye on the circle or the spiral." They did not look to realism but "a symphony of pattern with botanical variations, a transposition far removed from nature." Art Nouveau "concentrated the essence of flower, fish, bird and human forms, and transformed them into decorative symbols... Design, pattern and symbol became paramount."

Victorian and Edwardian Art Nouveau stained glass has ivy leaves trailing across borders; peacocks stretch long, languid feathers of brilliant hues, stylized flowers are scattered in flowing bouquets across windows and doors. These motifs lend themselves to the medium of glass. Their shapes can be curved and flattened to suit the material, and designed into ornate arrangements that complement the shape of a transom, or soften the rectangle of a window.

These designs are perennially popular, not only for their suitability to glass art, but because fruit, plants, and birds are comforting domestic motifs.

But abstract designs can give the glass artist great satisfaction. Pure shape, given significance through color, but transformed and altered by the vagaries of light, does express the abiding fascination of stained glass, and its essential quality of unpredictability.

Our technology offers us a wide range of options, and we are privileged to have, as personal craftsmen, a freedom from fashionable artistic styles. We can choose the sinuous line of Art Nouveau, or a geometric puzzle, or an abstract design to decorate our homes.

The Emotion of Color

We refer to color to describe states of mind. "She's blue today," "green with envy," or "in a black mood" are familiar emotional metaphors. When choosing colors for your glass design,

Far left The severity of the pointed-arch window is softened by the use of warm color and a joyous curving design.

Left This screen divides the hall and the kitchen. The glass used here has a very subtle surface texture, to add movement to the design. The view beyond is clearly visible from both sides. This increases the effect of openness and yet provides a clear division to the two areas.

Below A brightly lit room carries one window of subtle color made from slabs of agate and obsidian.

Below Commercial textured glass fused with translucent glass in a watery motif is used in a bathroom. Light and privacy are retained in the design.

Right The color scheme in this panel reflects the natural wood prevalent in the house. The use of a curved linear border softens the squareness of the window shape while the central area allows as much light into the room as possible.

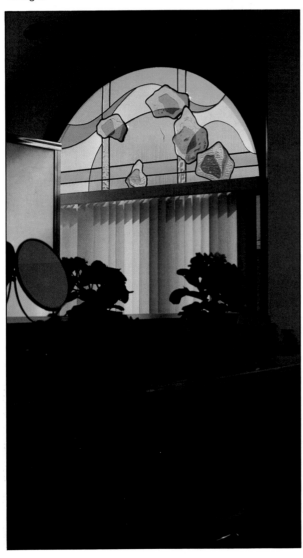

consider what effect various colors have upon your own perceptions, for color carries a high symbolic value.

When Gyorgy Kepes, professor of Visual Arts at The Massachussets Institute of Technology, was asked to design the stained glass windows for St. Mary's Cathedral in San Francisco, he relied on this symbolism to express the four elements of life: air and light were represented by gold; for earth, Kepes used green, and a rich mixture of rubies and oranges indicated fire; blue was for water. These windows have been hailed for their breathtaking combination of sunlight and color that glows "in a manner that rivals medieval cathedrals."

What combinations would suit your home? Do you like cool, clean tones or sludgy, subtle shades? You may choose to express different moods in different rooms, preferring to move from a serene atmosphere to a vibrant cheerfulness, and on to deeper shadiness. Or this kind of change may create a sense of uneasiness within you, and you find that a gentle balance of color will bring you a sense of peace. The colors that surround you will affect you, and it is reassuring and exciting to understand how colors work and how you respond to them. Through stained glass, colored light assumes a tension and a vibrancy. Its effect will work upon the design of the window and the colors in your room. The light should penetrate your stained glass so that it sits compatibly with your furnishings.

When you have decided upon the colors that will suit you and the interiors of your home, analyze how color works. Put one shade against another, red close to blue, and the light will shimmer and blur into purple. Is purple light the color you want? Look at the great examples of glass art and learn from their color combinations. Hold colors together and experiment before making a decision and cutting

Below The glass artist has boldly obscured the center with deep color yet he has allowed daylight to predominate.

your precious glass. The symbolic value of color will help you create the atmosphere. Rich, warm, earthy golds and greens may suit your kitchen, or a pattern of pastel and white light to soothe the baby's room. Let the color describe the emotional atmosphere of your home.

Glass Spaces

There are surprising and unexpected areas where stained glass adds a startling dimension. An internal wall can be broken by the introduction of a glass panel. The play of light between one room and the other will create an exciting, glowing glass panel, and electricity will provoke a mysterious vibrancy. A rich and complex design in stained glass can be used in this way.

On an entrance door, the design should be a grammar of welcome, inviting the guest with a promise of the home within, and pleasing the stranger who simply passes by. Such a door is often designed with glass because natural light is a necessity within, and it is important to consider this when planning your stained glass window. A *grilles* may be the best solution, involving, as it does, a combination of colored and white light. Frank Lloyd Wright was a master in this approach to stained glass usage, as was Charles Rennie Mackintosh, the Scottish architect and designer whose aesthetics had such a profound influence all over Europe at the end of the last century. Both these men devised delicate linear use of stained glass motifs to intersect and enhance areas of natural light.

There are entrance doors that are designed

Right A typical hallway in a London house dating from 1906.

Below This entrance door had lost its original glass so the design has been entirely made up to be in keeping with the Edwardian style.

specifically to carry stained glass, which becomes an important element both in the facade and in the interior. Such doors permit a powerful use of stained glass work, and the design should be of a quality dramatic enough to serve as a focal point from the street view, and to cause a glowing shimmer of colored light within the house. If you are planning such a door, allow a mix of textures, and fine contrasts of rich and pale color tones.

The Japanese prefer not to put doors in their homes and in this way avoid the claustrophobia of closed in areas. But we use doors in our architecture, and an imaginative insertion of decorative stained glass will introduce a light and airy effect to the usual dull blankness of an internal door. Narrow panels can modify the barrier of a door, and a delicate *grilles* can have an astounding

effect in creating a sense of space within a house, without any major reconstruction. And privacy can be maintained even as you transform the door and the space, by the use of a rich total design.

The usual solution to the dullness of internal doors is to place a transom between door and ceiling. Such spaces can provide the opportunity of using complex and ornate patterns designed to be a decorative feature more than a source of light. The color of the surrounding walls, and the electric lighting should be planned to carry the eye upwards towards this decorative panel.

Many homes have odd angles or neglected corners that can be given new character with stained glass. An imaginative and daring eye will find such spots. A long passage, which has all the appeal of a tunnel, will be transformed by the introduction of a stained glass window. Depending on the height at which this window is used, the design will not be noticed but the colored light will be important. Do you want a shaft of color falling from roof height? Or, alternatively, place your window two feet from ground level and create a pool of rainbow light.

Use stained glass in the roof. Perhaps a loft conversion becomes an eccentric delight simply because the craftsman had the nerve to insert colored glass into the roofing. This kind of nerve

Below A skylight window in an Art Deco study introduces a cool light to a narrow room. The clear colors suit the decor and purpose of this area.

Right These medallions fitted stylishly into French doors express the color mood and furnishings within. Stained glass doors can be symbolic of the ambience of the home.

Left This screen serves a functional need for privacy. This practical usage is expressed in the monotone, graphic quality of the design.

offers a design solution to the small, even poky, extension created for a kitchenette or bathroom. And the shower unit need not be encased by an unimaginative enclosure, just serving its purpose, but by a beautiful, decorative affair of stained glass, constantly changing as steam and water play across the color. Look at other "useful" aspects of your interior decor. Would a divider between kitchen and living room add an important dimension to your apartment? Can your stairwell be improved?

Of course, major decisions to build enclosures or dividers, or even creating or replacing windows, may be inhibited by the cost of fitting them. There are design solutions that need not cost too much. A stained glass screen makes an exquisite divider, and gives exciting scope for the craft of glass art. Tiffany designed one for the White House in Washington, using eagles as an emblem. Sadly, it has been broken up and lost to us.

A screen can be moved at will, and the color effects can be constantly, subtly changed by placing it before different sources of light. The very nature of glass makes it an ideal material for use as a divider or a screen. It serves its purpose in creating areas of privacy, yet the light effects prevent it from assuming the character of a barrier.

If it is not possible to remove your old windows, hang panels of stained glass over them. These panels can be suspended and stabilized with chains. Design a series of panels that can be fitted as shutters across the windows. This design resolution gives you the option of playing with the effects of colored light, using it when the natural light is not pleasing or necessary, or folding it away just as you wish.

There is no reason to be inhibited or conventional in your own private space. Your craftsmanship is an important statement of your individuality and imaginative expression in a world that threatens to overwhelm us with fashionable consumerism or mediocre styles for the "average person."

References
H. Weber Wilson, *Great Glass in American Architecture.* Tessa Paul, *The Art of Louis Comfort Tiffany,* Quintet 1987.

CHAPTER 2

Right Tiffany lamps were created to counteract the harsh glare of electric light. Diffused through glorious stained glass this light becomes warm and vibrant.

Above A lamp that follows the path of Art Nouveau designers who decorated the new electricity in familiar female and plant forms.

A ny and every building is a protective structure, a device to ward off the cold, the rain, the wind, and the dust, yet one element must be allowed entrance, the noble phenomenon of light. Architects must arrange to trap and capture light without disturbing the purpose of the building. Walls are built with small gaps, long narrow spaces, great circular holes, all manner of spaces to allow daylight to penetrate the interior. The earliest builders and architects began to play with light. Long shafts of sunbeam were directed to sharpen the important features of a room, or the light was turned away to dissolve with dark shadow a crisp right-angle. Light began to assume a symbolic value, and windows were arranged to significant effect. Perhaps the most powerful, yet most simple, demonstration of the symbolic use of light is found in the early Buddhist "stupas." Spiro Kostof in his *History of Architecture* describes the journey of Buddhist pilgrims when they entered the dark, narrow passage leading to their ultimate place of worship. As they felt their way along, "the darkness thickened at every step: the certainties of time and space elapsed. Then at the edge of the fathomless, the dome of the stupa glowed suddenly, as if the cosmic egg was being unveiled in the heart of the earth. The source of the light was, in actuality, a hole at the top of the rock shell."

Kostof writes, also, of the use of light in the Alhambra, that supreme architectural expression of Moorish Spain. "There are no openings at all to the outside wall at eye level... Light is courted with, absorbed. No sharp definition of shade is allowed, and a soft, languid, liquid atmosphere is created where mass is not entirely palpable, and the space is not entirely void."

Christian architecture evolved into interiors of

Below Light shades of stained glass are gorgeous but the lamp base is significant too. Here a decorative metal stand echoes themes from the shade.

Right Restrained use of color and a clean simplicity of form creates a warm glow of color, without the exuberance of a more ornate color combination.

richly refractive light-filled effects and with an intricate symbolism of light, often emphasized by the use of stained glass. In many ways, in many cultures, daylight was used as a tool to color and paint the interiors of buildings.

Met by Moonlight

Light within a building in the dark hours of night presents an entirely different problem. For long centuries, we relied on fire to dispel the night, and this source of light can be moved from room to room, or its position can be altered within one room. This mobility made any calculation of light effects an impossible task for architects. The style of the building, its internal ambience, was beyond their control at night. It became the purpose of the craftsmen who made the holders and containers of firelight, to give these objects, but not the light, a symbolic value.

Much ingenuity went into designing containers to hold the firelight. All sorts of things were invented: sconces, oil lamps, brackets, candlesticks, lanterns, candelabra, and chandeliers. Inevitably, great artistic skill began to make strange and lovely designs to transform the purely functional. Magical attributes were given, eventually, to the *objet* that carried the light. The old fairy tale of *Aladdin and The Lamp* demonstrates dual attitudes to the lamp. In this story, the boy appreciates the domestic value of the lamp, and longs for a new one to display in his home, but the lamp has a fantasy value, too. It not only offers light, but lo! it carries a dream world within itself.

The craftsmen felt this ambivalence, and the fire holders were decorated to demonstrate their nonfunctional value. Candlesticks for use in churches carried motifs of religious belief and holy

Below The shape of the iris is given a new significance in a design that makes a bold interpretation of a favorite Art Nouveau theme.

emblems. Often, they were made tall and impressive, to lift and spread the light through the church, and immense candles were fitted into them. They were wrought in precious metals, and in glass, although the earliest use of glass for the purpose of carrying light was in Syria of the thirteenth and fourteenth centuries. Little glass lanterns were made in the Middle East at that time. These so called "mosque lamps" were exquisitely enameled and gilded with quotations from the Koran in flowing calligraphy. These lanterns were suspended from the ceiling and secured by loops of chain. The Islamic aesthetic, with its passion for intricate, repetitive patterns, created lanterns of complex "lace" work in brass and gold and clay, as well as glass, and delighted in the patterns that the light within created upon the surfaces without. The early lanterns of Europe were more prosaic in their arrangements, being built as sturdy boxes to protect

Below Contemporary designs in light shades prefer a restrained use of pattern and color. Traditional rich patterning may often be at variance with the function of a modern room.

Below right This lamp shade uses rich tones of color to compensate for a simplicity of design. Reds and oranges used in warm shades enhance this design.

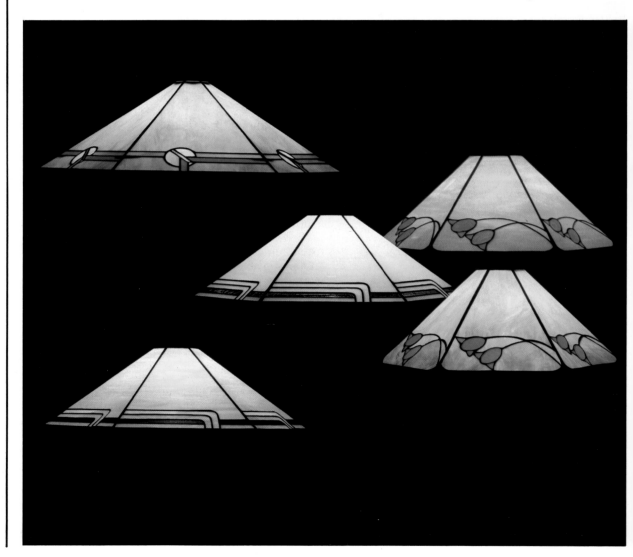

Left An original handling of the lamp edge is demonstrated in this example of a hanging lamp with unexpected details adding emphatic decoration.

the flame. They were generally used to light dark passages or were for external use.

However, these became more ornate and developed later into table lamps, when in 1784, the Argeund lamp was invented. This allowed a more efficient use of oil flow to the wick, and the flame was fitted with a glass tube. Porcelain and etched glass were favorite materials in the production of these, although brass was widely used among the less wealthy. By 1850, such oil lamps were in widespread use, and "frosted" glass tubes became popular.

Despite these advances in oil lamps, the use of candlelight was not abandoned. Candelabra, with two or more arms, acting as candle sockets, become more ornate in design, and especially flamboyant when designed in glass. Cut surfaces and numerous pendant drops flashed and reflected the candle flames in a very pretty manner. Chandeliers did not lose favor either, and, as a material, glass was preferred by designers because of its reflective quality. The Venetians made the first glass chandeliers in the eighteenth century, and these "light-holders" became more and more elaborate in design, until, in the Victorian era they had the appearance of shimmering glass waterfalls.

As with all *objets*, the light holder became a desirable item, denoting through material and design, the wealth, the status, or the faith of its owner. But it was rarely an architectural feature, and remained in the realm of craftsmen. Massive chandeliers may occasionally have been regarded as a detail worth the architect's attention, because these could be "fixed" into place on ceilings.

The light source was not, of course, always portable, but was fixed not only as chandeliers, but as sconces and brackets on the wall. Different levels of light offered new effects to the low brilliance of

Below Tiffany produced the famous dragon-fly design. Richly colored, the insect was caught in a flight of fantasy shapes.

The Light of Science

William Murdoch of Great Britain is usually given credit for being the first to apply coal gas on any considerable scale. He set up a small experimental plant in 1795, and by 1815, Westminster Bridge in London was lit by gas lamps.

However, although Murdoch's experiments brought a radical change in fuel systems, the quality of light was not altogether different from that of candlelight or oil. Gas burns with a yellowish luminous flame, which yet has a softening and gentle effect. Craftsmen simply adapted their skills to the mechanical design requirements of gas fittings, but generally imitated the design of the oil lamps with similar glass tubes. It was in the making of gas street lamps that design became interesting and very ornamental.

It was the advent of electricity that revolutionized the use of light in architecture and radically altered the demands on craftsmen who fashioned the new electric lamps. In the 1880s, after Thomas Edison had perfected a system to transmit and distribute electrical energy, the novelty and convenience of the system enchanted the consumer. But electric light has a harsh and brutal glare, and when Louis Comfort Tiffany was asked to design the interior of the first theater to be lit by electricity, he questioned the considerable brightness of this lighting system. When the Lyceum Theatre opened in 1885 in New York, the audience were greeted by light softly shaded through green glass. And so, Mr. Tiffany, who devoted his life to the twin obsessions of color and light, resolved the problem of the fierce brightness of electricity by transmitting it through colored glass.

Tiffany Lamps

Tiffany's design solution to the quality of electri-

candlelight, and these wall fittings sometimes carried flames of fire that increased clarity and visibility within the nighttime interior. But for an architect, fire or nightlight was both predictable and eccentric, and of such a nature that any attempt to modify its effects was both worthless and unnecessary as a design consideration.

There was no need to seek protection from candle or oil light. The light from a candle is soft, mellow, even dim. It causes long shadows, or draws a deep inky darkness that softly edges the wavering circle of light. Such a light carried mystery and subtlety, and it is gentle in tone. Then, in the nineteenth century, that momentous century, new sources of light were discovered that demanded innovative responses from artist and architect alike.

Left The decorative beauty of a "Tiffany" lamp enhances any room. In this space the lamp assumes the importance of an objet d'art when placed with a series of fine paintings.

Above Shimmering glass adds a touch of frivolity to the functional lamp shape, making it a suitable partner to the languid lamp shade.

Right The vibrant colors of the parrot's feathers contrast with the simplicity of the Art Deco style wall lamps.

Below Modern art glaziers prefer to take a bolder approach to design than earlier designers. This floral theme is far less elaborate than its Art Nouveau antecedents.

city caused a sensation in lamp design and his own stained glass lamps became so popular, that "Tiffany lamp" became a generic term.

Louis Comfort Tiffany sought, with his glass shades, to repeat the mellow and gentle effects of the old candle, oil, and gas systems; but he also siezed the opportunity to create a new design motif. As a young man he had traveled extensively in the East, and he always showed a predilection for the style of the Orient. He had been tremendously excited by the glass mosaics, and the faiences used all over the Arab world, and collected an enormous quantity of "domestic wares" on his travels. His vast personal wealth allowed him to buy textiles, carpets, tiles, dishes, swords, and lamps. On his return to the United States, his interior designs for some of the most distinguished residences (including the White House) were opulent with Islamic inspired, richly ornate patterns, objects, and furniture.

Confronted by the prosaic quality of electric light, he contrived to give it a luxurious charm with stained glass, perhaps to repeat the beauty of Arabic lamps. Tiffany lamps were shaded by domed "roofs" built from a rainbow mosaic of glass. Electric light was subdued to a romantic shimmer through the transforming magic of colored glass.

He created glass "mosaics" in an Oriental manner surrounding tiny pieces of colored glass in a tight web of cames. With his abiding love of natural forms, he used the motifs of the Art Nouveau style, fruits, flowers, and leaves tumbled over his shades. The designs were contrived to express the shape of the shade. Wisteria blossoms fell into an easy, circular rhythm; thick clusters of grapes created a curled edging. All were made of brilliant colors. The light penetrated the blossoms and tendrils to make patterned effects of graduated colored light on the

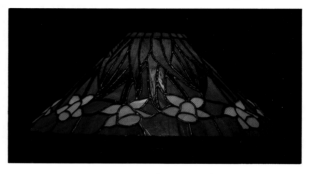

Below A daring use of primary colors and an emphatic use of cames have created a glowing source of light in this ornamental standing lamp.

walls and furnishings.

American homes all over the country had at least one corner where a Tiffany lamp, or an imitation, made a warm, artistic glow in the evenings. The leaded glass shades were not an innovation from the Tiffany Studios, but his designs were far superior to any other similar product. "Louis Tiffany held a comprehensive knowledge of the effects of light, transmitted and reflected. He considered the harshness of electricity, and softened the glare with lovely colour. He also gave technical consideration to his designs. The electric lamps were given armatures to alter the focus of light. Shades could be interchangeable. Tiffany combined function with aesthetic appeal in these lamps."

Design Alternatives

The new light brought a whole range of problems to architecture. Night light could now be controlled and measured and utilized as an important aspect in the design of buildings. Architects perceived new ways of emphasizing an angle or creating a recess by careful use of electric light. Buildings could be given an extended usage as electricity meant the building could be utilized efficiently during the night.

A hundred years after the invention of electricity,

Below The furniture relies on the elegance and sheen of wood. The visual focus is in the vibrant stained glass lamp of strong colors.

Right A lyrical design of roses in this Tiffany-type design depends on a gentle mix of color hues.

light fittings remain a challenge to designers. A single bulb in the middle of a room is a logical fitting as light can then be spread around the entire space, but visually, the hanging central light can be ugly and obtrusive. A fitting placed at a certain angle can create problems by casting unwanted shadows, or throwing a light on to a wall that reflects and dazzles. An ill-lit passage becomes, at night, a vaguely sinister area, even in your own home.

The early designers were absorbed by the design problems of electricity. Shades were the great innovation, but so were stands and bases. There was even, indeed there still is, a refusal to conceive new forms to hold the new light. The traditional candlestick was simply adapted to hold an electric light bulb. This solution was applied even to chandeliers, despite the fact that light bulbs sat awkward and ugly in the old candle sockets. But many craftsmen, especially the Art Nouveau designers, devised new and extraordinary appliances to carry electricity.

From this early twentieth-century excitement, came sinuous designs in metal. Freed from the design inhibitions of candle and oil holders, the craftsmen made some odd statements. Languid female figures would hold a glass ball from which the electricity glowed; male athletes were contorted into discus throwers, the discus being the light bulb. One of the more pleasing of these ill-suited concepts is the lamp designed by Gustav Gurschner for the Loetz glass factory in Austria. Dated 1900, a slender female molds herself into a tall, standing, curvilinear metal mount, topped by a semi-globe of iridescent glass. Once again, the work from the Tiffany Studios was of a superior quality. Under Tiffany's transforming hand, the stands and bases for his lamps became works of art.

Initially, he used bronze to make bases. He

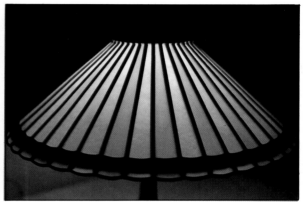

Below The glazier has crafted a glass shade of severe spokes softened with slightly curved outer rims. The golden light is used to emphasize the stark design.

sometimes used Byzantine designs, giving the metal an antique appearance. "The organic shapes of nature — leaves, tendrils, cobwebs, roots of trees — became models for curving, sculptural forms." An extravagant shade of grapes and leaves is supported by a plain bronze stem, simulating the texture of wood. Or he would repeat the curved shape of the shade with ornate metal work. When using ceramics, he emphasized the color and texture of that material and matched it with a simple, mono-colored shade.

Tiffany's floor lamps are remarkably functional and modern in design. One example is a tall bronze column, set upon angled legs, which has a globe constructed of metal strips between which black glass is set. The light is transmitted in a greenish shimmer. It is purely functional in its shape, and gains its decorative status from the unusual lighting.

By 1920, electric light fittings were generally improving in both function and elegance. From the Bauhaus design school in Germany, lamps of wonderful simplicity were being designed, such as a very plain, very utilitarian, adjustable ceiling lamp from Marianna Brandt and Hans Przyembel in 1927. In the same year, Poul Henningsen produced a severely practical lamp in bronze and brass for Louis Poulsen in Copenhagen. But, by this time, the use of electricity had become a habit; people were used to its harsh light. Designers were planning round that brightness, incorporating it into their designs.

Perhaps it is only now, in the latter part of our century, that we appreciate again the softness and beauty of electricity transformed by colored glass. Like Tiffany and his colleagues, we long for the decorative effect of light falling through colored glass.

Light Concerns

Every homemaker is faced with the dilemma that any architect or designer confronts while planning a lighting system, which is that a duality of purpose must be expressed. The purpose of the light must be combined with the beauty and symbolic value of that light.

Overhead or ceiling lights are usually installed in

Below The wide circumference of this lamp spreads a wide pool of bright light, but the deep, rich border casts subtle color against the wall.

Right Butterflies and marble combine in a nostalgic Edwardian mix. Any sentimental excess is stopped by the clever use of abstract art glass.

every room, despite the fact that such clarity may not be required very often in certain areas. It is convenient to use one switch to light up one area instantly, and the switch itself should be fitted in a convenient area near the entrance to that room.

Wall lights are softer in effect than the ceiling light, and the wall creates a tension between itself and the light, which can be very pleasing. Such lights can also be used to emphasize a painting, or to enhance a mirror. The effect of light must be considered in relation to wall decorations. Should the light shine blankly on a painting, or reflect off the glass covering that painting, the effect will negate the purpose of the light. Careful consideration is needed when hanging pictures near wall lights.

Our choice of lighting systems is bewildering. There are strip lights, lights which are recessed into the wall, lights to use for cosmetic reasons, spot lights, lamp lights, floor lights, desk lamps. Our choice of design is enormous and varies from antique-type chandeliers to sleek, minimal structures of steel and plastic.

If possible, try some experiments in the effect of light on the shape of your room and the placing of your furniture. See where the shadows fall, because these can make the space look smaller, or your favorite chair may vanish in a sudden pool of darkness. There are different light requirements for different rooms, and each room will look different in electric light. Colors can change their tone, becoming darker or brighter or paler, and assume a significance that may be quite unexpected.

Do you understand how you use your home? At the beginning, new furniture and paint and drapes are chosen with loving care and with the purpose of creating a lovely environment. But as family life settles in and spreads itself, that lovely environment

will change. Each inhabitant will make their subtle demands, and they will adjust various areas and place certain objects to suit their individual needs.

Imperceptibly, the inanimate objects in the home move and change. A chair has been dragged nearer to a lamp, while a table has crept towards the natural light. Unexpected gifts, new purchases take up space assigned to the original ornaments. Your living area needs to be understood in terms of the comfort, and the ease, with which people use it.

Light is of supreme importance. Where are the working areas and do they need a bright, sharp light? Are there any favorite places for reading books? Do the children need a night light? How should the entrance be lit, or the patio?

These considerations are brisk, sensible and necessary, but then notions of beauty, privacy, intimacy, hospitality will attach themselves subtly to the sensible list of functions and these things will

affect your choice. The shape and color of the lighting appliance has to suit your room color and decor. It must not jar with your furniture. The design must suit the purpose. A banker's lamp will sit comfortably on a desk; a spotlight is perfect in the hobby room. But it is possible to make a glamorous choice in your lighting arrangements, a fitting that serves as a focal decorative point both in the day and when lit up at night.

Gorgeous Light

Tiffany lamps, or stained glass lamps, are the most gorgeous way to display light. Nobody can pretend they are a practical form of lighting, but they do offer supreme visual pleasure, as the light glitters through a tapestry of color, leaving a rich mantle of light on all the surrounding space and surfaces. In the lounge, a stained glass lamp is a major decorative feature. Not only will it create a warm serene light, conducive to conversation, but will delight the eye. In this room you have the opportunity to use standing lamps to great effect.

In the dining area, where it does not do to have a light so dim that eating becomes a difficult act, or a harsh brightness that has an alarming effect on the mood of the diners, stained glass has a soothing effect. Wall lights, or a lamp on the table as a decorative feature in the meal setting, should be considered. The bedroom and the bathroom are considerably improved by the light of stained glass. Depending on your design, and the colors you choose, an intimate or sensuous mood can be created by an ornamental stained glass light. And for nightlights in the nursery, a small stained glass lamp of reassuring colors can both calm and fascinate a child.

Be bold and imaginative with your stained glass lamp. Just as the vast works of the great glaziers

Below left The glass artist has concentrated color in a close floral pattern at the top of this lamp, allowing a wider spread of clear light around the room interior.

Below right Daylight and artificial light are exploited by placing this stained glass lamp near the window.

Right The dining area is lit by stained glass but the use of milky translucent material ensures a clear light over the table.

were observed and studied for their design, color and light effects in windows, so a study of lamps by Tiffany, or Frank Lloyd Wright will help when designing your shade.

Ornamental Effects

Stained glass windows are affected by the eccentricities of natural light, but in lamps, the light is controlled and its intensity can be properly taken into account when choosing colors and designs. Natural forms are very suitable in Tiffany lamps. Not only do the motifs fit themselves easily into the circular or conical shape of the shade, but the colors can be justifiably spectacular. The dark pink of rose, with ivy green, a touch of navy and perhaps a space of clear light; or russet reds and oranges, caramel browns and nut colors; these amazing combinations suit a motif of leaves, fruit, and birds. Tiffany used dragonflies and peacocks for their ornamental shape as well as their colors.

The electric light will burn steadily, and, for this reason, very rich colors will produce a jewel-like effect. A lamp that is designed for this effect should be planned as ornamental rather than functional, except if used as a standing lamp. Then the shade

will be lifted as a visual statement, while the light falls white on the area below.

Frank Lloyd Wright tended to use geometric shapes, creating angular shades with four corners. His stained glass lamps are surprisingly modern in design. He also uses a more translucent light effect, not being as fond as Tiffany was of opulent colored glass.

Art Deco, with its emphasis on angles and "chevron" approach to design is often a suitable style for wall lights. But again, modified shapes from nature such as shells, or the cone of a lily, make fine design ideas for wall lamps. It is better not to use dark or rich colors, as such tones would certainly be at variance with the function of the light.

There are no definite laws governing the choice of design in your stained glass lamp, apart from the

Below The austere angular base of this desk lamp is a foil to the rich geometry of the shade.

usual parameters set by glass. One of the great delights of stained glass work is to take any design or color, pattern or painting, and, through the glowing iridescence of colored glass, transform the design model. Geometric, or Art Nouveau, landscape or abstract, the stained glass will metamorphize the color and effect as no other medium can. Electric light will fall through your stained glass with a dynamic vibrancy, and with a thrilling color effect.

Basics

Because stained glass lamps can be so patently ornamental, the designer tends to neglect the base. There is one approach to this design problem that claims that a very simple base is best suited to the ornate shade. As we know, Louis Comfort Tiffany did not approve this approach. Indeed, all the

master craftsmen try to synchronize and harmonize all parts of the *objet* they are creating.

It is still possible to find quaint and unusual lamp bases in flea markets and antique stalls. Despite the fact that these may be very decorative, do not dismiss them as possible bases for a stained glass shade. Perhaps the design of the base can be recreated in the glass shade; or an abstract stained glass design using the colors of the base may create a harmonious color solution.

Heavy, old brass candlesticks carry the great curved beauty of a stained glass shade. The design of such a base may allow for a very grand design, perhaps with an irregular edge to the shade, such as the edge of the famous Wisteria Lamp from the Tiffany Studios. An austere, simple candlestick is well suited to a purely abstract design.

Right The room is serene and subdued in color but the art glass of the lamp introduces an element of vitality.

Below Light falls through the stained glass creating gold from orange.

Modern Japanese design can be beautifully translated into a stained glass lamp. A stylish use of black base, with a mixed use of red and blacks and clear glass in the stained glass shade, will add an elegant decorative feature to the clean, straight lines of modern furniture design. Many department stores carry square vases made in bright porcelains of colors so firm, navy blue, pillar box red, a high white, that they appear to be lacquered. These hard, shiny colors presented in a severe shape, look very well carrying stained glass shades, whether a floral motif or an abstract design is used in the glass.

A stained glass lamp makes an important visual statement in your home and, for this reason, the base should be worthy of the decoration.

Shades for Floor Lamps

Floor lamps permit a great deal of design freedom. Here, the use of light at such a low level is intrinsically for design effect. The shape of the lamp and the light it casts are only to create a pleasing decorative effect and, for this reason, stained glass is the perfect medium.

It offers the opportunity for arresting decoration. A rich weave of colors, a beautiful motif of leaves, irises, feathers, whatever can be woven into a lyrical pattern, is permissible at this level. A stark, geometric or a "paper cut-out" design will create a modern sculpture effect. Another model is the old Oriental brass lamp, with its intricate interwoven design, with spaces to allow the light out. Pattern your stained glass on this lacy effect, for a spectacular use of light and color.

Of course, the effect of light falling through the colored glass will be of prime concern, even in floor lamps where the light is not expected to be clear and bright. In a floor lamp, the light will be an important part of a powerful visual statement.

Left This hanging light is unusual in design but complementary to the kitchen decor.

Lantern-Lit

Lanterns, by implication, are for external use, and the use of stained glass should be employed with circumspection. A lantern of brilliant hue hanging from your front door may make a dubious statement!

On a back porch or on patios, a stained glass lantern can be quite different in its statement. A summer evening, lit by a series of little jewel-like lanterns, can assume magical proportions as they glow in the soft night air. A large lantern, or two, makes for a festive air of partying pleasure.

With an outdoor lantern on your patio, you may prefer to revert to candlelight, but remember if you do plan to use candles, the light will not be bright, so design a lantern to use on the table not the wall and have a gentle, mysterious glow to hold off the darkness.

This is Your Light

The design of your stained glass lamp, as in your stained glass window or door or screen is *your* statement of your artistic and emotional needs.

Sketch flowers, leaves, or butterflies; find your favorite shapes, or copy the work of admired artists and craftsmen. A motif on a little porcelain cup picked up in a junk shop, or something a child has drawn with naive charm; your favorite scarf, or fabric, or something that has a particular significance for your home such as the family cat or the canary — all these can be transformed into a design that will make your stained glass your very own expression of craftsmanship.

The traditional methods of working with stained glass require very few specialized tools. Simple techniques, practiced and carried out with confidence will allow you to create a wide variety of projects with a professional looking finish.

Lead glazing or leaded glass is the traditional way of assembling stained, or more accurately, colored glass. The same basic technique has been used for centuries and even today most commercially-made stained glass windows are produced in this way. Lead is used as the jointing material because of its malleability and low cost compared to other metals.

This technique of assembling glass panels consists of cutting pieces of glass to shape and inserting them into strips of channeled lead called *came*. This term comes from an old English word "calme" meaning "string" or "length." The lead is cut to the required lengths and soldered together at the points where they meet to form an integrated section or panel. It is impractical to construct large panels of glass as single units because, without intermediate structural supports, they would be liable to collapse from their own weight and they would have little resistance to damage from wind pressure. For this reason, large areas of leaded glass are made up of several smaller sections, each of a manageable size and weight. For extra strength, metal bars corresponding to the outline of the sections are set into the supporting framework and the panel is tied to them with copper wire. In this way, the weight of the window is supported at intervals and is firmly secured to the fabric of the building.

When all the joints have been soldered on both sides, the panel is strengthened further and weatherproofed by filling the small gaps between the glass surface and the lead with a linseed oil putty cement. After the final cleaning, the panel is ready for installation.

For delicate work it is often better to use the later technique of copper foiling, which can be used equally well for both two- and three-dimensional objects. This technique is particularly suitable for boxes, terraria, and lamp shades. One particular advantage of copper foil is that many smaller pieces can be soldered together to create intricate detail that is impossible even with the very finest lead came. Copper foil is also ideally suited to the technique of "plating" glass, which is the laying together of two or more pieces of glass for strength, protection, and a wide range of visual effects and color variations.

Copper foil, which is generally purchased in pre-cut adhesive-backed rolls, is available in widths of $3/16$-$1/2$ inch (4-12 mm). Foil is also available in sheet form for masking filigree work. A new development has created black-backed and silvered copper foil, which can be used for variety and striking visual effect. The narrower the foil, the thinner the resulting joints in the design, and the more delicate the appearance of the finished object. When using foil, particular attention must be paid to accuracy when cutting the glass, since it is important that each piece of glass fits snugly with its neighbor. Any minor bumps and hollows along the edge of the glass will be magnified once the foil has been applied and the pieces are set against each other.

Assembling colored glass projects using copper foil to secure the glass in position is slightly different from using lead. Once the glass is cut, each piece is wrapped along its edge with a thin strip of foil. The foil is centered on the edge and then flattened securely onto the face of the glass. The wrapped pieces are arranged in position and tacked together at strategic points with blobs of solder. Molten solder is drawn along the seams with a hot soldering iron and left to cool, leaving the pieces of glass securely joined by a neatly-rounded bead of solder.

When a curved surface such as a lamp shade is being constructed, the individual pieces are usually set on a mold and soldered in place at the correct angle. Once soldered together, the glass pieces form a rigid structure that cannot be bent into an alternative shape. Foiling is used more widely in the United States, but with the increasing availability of supplies, it is becoming more popular in Europe.

There are various other methods that can be used to construct stained glass panels, for instance, using dalle-de-verre — glass made in thick slab form. This was developed in France in the 1930s. However, the traditional method of lead glazing and the more recent use of copper foil are still the most common techniques for working with colored glass. The first stage in producing a stained glass window is to make

TECHNIQUES

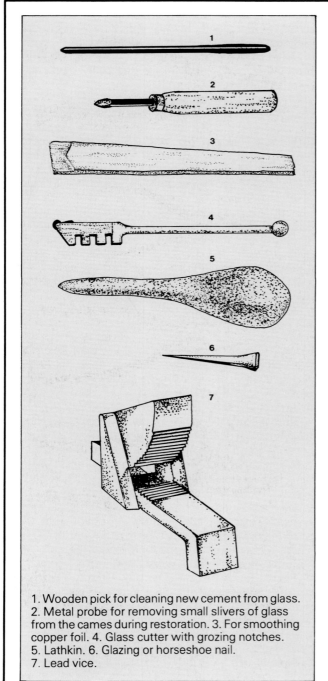

1. Wooden pick for cleaning new cement from glass.
2. Metal probe for removing small slivers of glass from the cames during restoration. 3. For smoothing copper foil. 4. Glass cutter with grozing notches.
5. Lathkin. 6. Glazing or horseshoe nail.
7. Lead vice.

a scale drawing on paper. Once the sketch is finalized the design is scaled up into a full size pattern or cartoon to cut the glass against. Basic drawing tools are all that are required at this stage, a ruler, paper, and pencil will suffice. A flat surface the size of the finished panel and good light will make the job easier. When the design is drawn to full size you will need a sheet of tracing paper and a felt-tipped pen that produces a line equal to the inside dimension of the lead. You may wish to include colored crayons or watercolors to the above list to give you a better idea of what the finished panel will look like.

Cutting the glass to shape requires a special glass cutting tool with either a diamond tip or a tungsten carbide wheel to score the surface of the glass. This produces a weakness in the structure of the glass along the score line.

The diamond cutter is best suited to cutting straight lines and is consequently impractical for many of the shapes used in stained glass work. The best tool for the stained glass craftsman is a glass cutter fitted with a tungsten carbide wheel. A good basic cutter consists of four parts: the shaft, the cutting wheel, grozing notches, and the finger rest. Some cutters have replaceable cutting wheels and are equipped with a weighted ball end for "tapping the score." Grozing notches are used for nibbling the edge of the glass to the desired shape. Between cuts, the cutter should be dipped in a light machine oil to lubricate and prolong the life of the wheel. When not in use, it should be stored in a small screw-top jar containing an absorbent pad that has been soaked in a mixture of two parts mineral spirits and one part light household oil.

There are glass-cutting saws available on the market that actually saw through the glass. These are generally used by professionals to produce highly complex shapes and would be an unnecessary expense for the hobbyist.

Pliers are used to make the process of breaking the glass easier and, whereas ordinary flat-nosed pliers are acceptable, there are pliers made specifically for breaking glass. There are three types available but the most versatile pliers have smooth flat jaws, top and bottom, and meet only at the very end. The jaws pinch the glass directly along the score line. Then, pressure is applied in a downward motion and the score opens up to produce the break.

Running pliers are a similar to glass breaking pliers and are furnished with a convex lower jaw and a concave upper jaw. They are applied to the edge of the glass at 90 degrees to the score. When the pliers are gently squeezed the score is forced apart. Better quality pliers have a screw stop adjustment to prevent the jaws from crushing the glass by closing too tightly.

The third type of pliers used in stained glass are called grozing or nibbling pliers. They are employed to chew thin slivers from the cut glass pieces that are slightly misshapen. The bottom jaw is concave, running to a chisel end that meets the flat end of the upper jaw . Pressure is applied in a similar fashion to the breaking pliers.

Having cut the glass, the next step is the leading process. Before it can be used the lead must be stretched, which both straightens and strengthens it. It is a simple operation that is performed by placing one end in a lead vice and pulling on the other. The first inch of lead is fed into the jaws of the vice and gripped by the serrated teeth. The vice, which should be securely mounted on the edge of a work bench, works in conjunction with gravity so that the more you pull on the lead, the tighter the grip becomes.

The channels of the lead are opened up by using a wooden stick called a lathkin. A lathkin is simply a smooth flat piece of hard wood approximately ¼ inch (6mm) thick tapered down to approximately ⅛ inch (3mm) at one end, but any piece of smooth, thin hard wood will do as a temporary measure. For example, an old wooden ruler or a piece of thin plywood would be suitable, as long as it is shaped and kept well polished. The lathkin is wedged into the channel and pulled along the entire length of the lead to open the channels of the came.

The prepared lead is cut to the desired length with a lead knife. These knives are available in two basic shapes, either chisel-ended or finished with a convex curve. Keep the steel blade sharp by regular use of an oilstone. Lead-knife handles are often weighted to act as a hammer for tapping leading

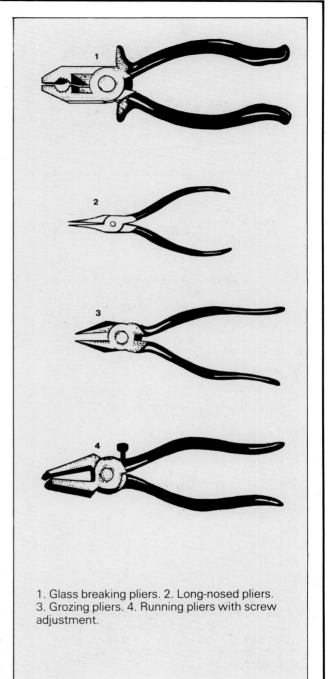

1. Glass breaking pliers. 2. Long-nosed pliers. 3. Grozing pliers. 4. Running pliers with screw adjustment.

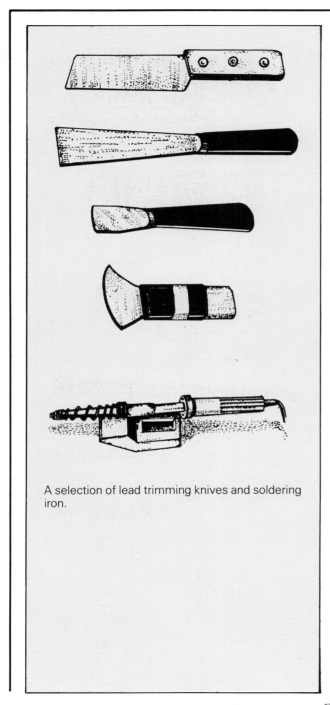

A selection of lead trimming knives and soldering iron.

nails into the production bench. As a temporary measure you could make a lead knife by cutting short an old-fashioned table knife and sharpening the blunt end.

An essential piece of equipment is the building board, which provides the surface to construct the panel on. This simply consists of a piece of particle board larger than the size of the finished panel with two battens fixed at the required angle to conform with the outline and dimensions of the work.

Leading or glazing nails are used to hold panes of glass and lead in position on the building board during construction. These nails are generally 1½-2 inches (35-50mm) long, square in section, with large square heads tapering smoothly to a point. However, if you cannot obtain suitable glazing nails, 2 inch (50mm) ovals will do as a substitute. Keep at least 20 nails handy while you work.

Once the entire panel has been leaded-up, the joints are secured with solder. Prior to the soldering, all the joints are cleaned with a small wire brush. Then the flux is applied to the joints to assist in the flow and bonding of the molten solder.

There are two types of soldering iron available, propane and electric, but propane irons are usually cumbersome to work with, making the electric irons the preferable choice. Electric soldering irons come in a range of sizes measured in watts. It's wise to get an iron with a rheostat temperature control that allows you to leave the iron plugged in for an extended period of time without the tip becoming overheated. The working end or tip is replaceable and should be wiped clean with a damp sponge frequently during use. This will prolong its life and assist the soldering process. Tips come in a variety of shapes and sizes and are either copper or iron-clad. Copper tips do yield better results but they are not as long lasting as iron-clad tips. The most common shapes are chisel, semi-chisel, and pyramid, which are available in both materials. A good all-purpose choice is chisel ended with a ⅜ inch (9mm) wide tip.

Once all the joints of the window have been soldered on both sides of the panel, then the final stage of cementing and cleaning can commence. Cement is forced into the small gap between the flanges of the lead came and the glass using a stiff bristled brush. The cement is left to dry and later the excess is picked out with a metal tool similar to a bradawl. To finish off, the glass is cleaned by rubbing a clean stiff-bristled brush vigorously across its surface.

In addition to these items, there are extra tools to assist the crafts person. These include a glass grinder, a stopping knife, and a light box. Glass grinders are particularly useful when working with copper foil because the precise fit of the individual pieces of glass is of particular importance. When you are working with lead, the flanges of the came cover any small irregularities on the edges of the glass. An ordinary workshop grinder can be used, however it requires a much more sensitive approach to prevent the glass from chipping. A grinder specifically designed for working with glass is constantly lubricated with running water that keeps the wheel clean and the glass cool to resist chipping. Generally, these are fitted with a diamond cutting-head, which will give between 150 and 200 hours of grinding time before it needs replacement.

A stopping knife has a thin, medium-length blade rounded at the end and turned up about an inch from the tip. The blade is always blunt and it is used, during the leading process, to lift pieces of glass up from the bench a fraction so they can be easily slid home into the channel of the lead came.

A light box or light table is a neatly packaged illuminated plate glass screen. It is useful for selecting glass during the design stage, and can be used to cut dark glass against a pattern. Although not essential to begin with, the light box is a valuable addition to the stained glass worker. It allows you to get a reasonably good idea of the effect of the glass panel before the project has been completed when alterations are difficult to make. Step-by-step instructions for making a simple light box are given on page 81.

All the tools mentioned above, except the lead knife and cementing brushes, are also used in conjunction with copper foil construction. The only tool specifically designed for copper foil work is the foil machine. This machine dispenses the foil from the roll, separates the backing paper, centers the foil on the edge of the glass, and folds the foil onto the surface of the glass. These edges should be finished off by hand with a lathkin.

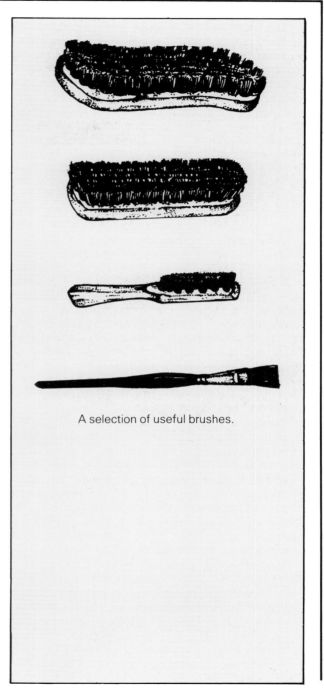

A selection of useful brushes.

The first and most important material is, of course, the glass itself. Choosing glass is always a pleasure because even in sheet form the exciting potential of the material is apparent to the artist. Sheet glass comes in a wide variety of textures and colors with every sheet having a character of its own. All stained glass is made up of sand, soda, potash, and metal oxides. These ingredients are heated together to approximately 2,500°F (1,370°C) where they combine in molten form to be machine processed or hand blown. There are two main types of glass available, machine made and hand blown, which is sometimes referred to as antique glass.

Machine-made glass is produced by extruding molten glass between two rollers. This glass, which is usually uniform in thickness, often has a surface texture embossed on one side during the rolling process. Rolled glass is available in two basic varieties—cathedral and opalescent. Cathedral glass is transparent and nonreflective so it requires a light source behind it to be appreciated. Minor irregularities in the glass add to the pleasing effect by mildly distorting the images seen through it. Cathedral glass is slightly harder than opalescent glass, which makes it a bit more difficult to score and break. The combination of colors and patterns available in cathedral glass make it particularly useful for creating door and window panels.

Opalescent glass is translucent and has a milky appearance that reflects, as well as transmits, light. It is the result of the mixture of two or more colors, and the density of the color affects the amount of light that is transmitted through the glass. Opalescent glass is often used in lamp shades because it can obscure the light fitting and bulb. The ability to reflect light also makes it ideal for situations where there is no light source to shine through the piece from behind.

Machine-made glass can be produced in large sheets and is therefore relatively inexpensive. Hand-blown glass, by comparison, is relatively expensive and much less likely to be uniform, due to the way in which it is made. Molten glass is taken up on a blowing rod by the glass blower and blown into a cylinder approximately 3 feet (900mm) long and 1 foot (300mm) in diameter. To convert the cylinder into a sheet, the ends are cut off and the soft glass

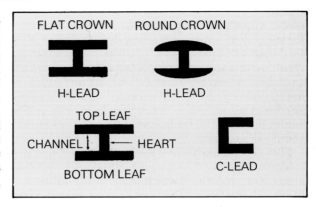

cylinder is cut along its length. The split cylinder is reheated in a kiln, opened out, and allowed to flatten on the kiln floor. This glass is sometimes termed antique glass and is of better quality than machined glass. The imperfections inherent in this type of production add to the overall character of the glass and any projects made from it. Some antique glass consists of two different colored layers. A thin "flashed" layer covers a thicker base layer. This glass can be etched with chemicals to erode the flashed layer revealing the base color. This process can be used to add further detail to a design.

The second most important material in stained glass construction is the jointing material. Lead comes in a variety of widths and is usually 6 feet (1.8m) in length. Most of the lead is channeled on both sides to accommodate adjoining panes of glass. This type of section is referred to as "H" lead. "C" lead, which is channeled on only one side, is used for perimeter work. Both lead types are available in round and flat profile. Cames are measured across the flanges for their width dimension, and across the channel for their height dimension. The center part of the came, which is called the heart, is also measured in both height and width. Some cames have a hole running the length of the heart to accommodate a thin strip of reinforcing steel. This steel strip adds rigidity to the panel without disrupting the overall design. Cames are also produced in copper, brass, and zinc for strength and aesthetic reasons.

Lengths of lead came are connected together with

solder applied to the joints. The most useful solder for stained glass work is an alloy of 60% tin and 40% lead and is termed "60/40." This ratio is important, resulting in a solder that reacts quickly yet hardens to make a strong joint. 60/40 solder melts at approximately 361°F (183°C) and the range between solid and molten state is roughly 13°F (70°C). The solder used should be the solid core variety ⅛ inch (3mm) in diameter.

Flux is a chemical used to clean the joint prior to soldering. It usually contains either oleic acid or ammonium chloride, which prevent the formation of metal oxides as the metals are heated. This provides a clean surface to ensure a solid bond between the solder and the jointing material. Flux can either be brushed on or rubbed on.

The most common alternative jointing material to lead is copper foil. It has an adhesive backing and comes in 36 yards (32m) long rolls in a variety of different widths. Copper foil is wrapped around each piece of glass prior to soldering. Once the pieces of glass have been wrapped with foil, they are butted together in position and molten solder is drawn along the entire seam. Copper foil has a great advantage over lead in three-dimensional projects because the glass can be positioned at any angle prior to soldering. Many Tiffany style lamps are fabricated using this method. They are assembled on a mold that is used to hold all the glass pieces in their relative positions at the correct angle while the lamp sections are being soldered.

The cement that fills in all the gaps between the glass and lead, making the panel weatherproof, is made from linseed oil putty thinned down with mineral spirits to a porridge-like consistency. Black powdered dye is often added to the cement to make it blend better with the lead came.

Finally, the excess cement is cleaned away from the surface of the workpiece with powdered chalk (whiting). This absorbs the moisture from the residual putty so that it can easily be brushed off.

In addition to these basic materials, there are a number of brass accessories and fittings used in the construction of lamps, boxes, and other projects. A variety of chemical applications, referred to as patinas, can be brushed on to alter the appearance of the solder or copper foil.

CEMENT RECIPE

75% Linseed oil putty
10% Mineral spirits
5% Linseed oil   Mixed
10% Lamp black
Whiting

Place the lamp black in a bucket. Slowly add the mineral spirits and linseed oil, mixing with a wooden spoon. When thoroughly blended, add the putty, a little at a time, ensuring that it is thoroughly blended before adding any more.
To adjust the consistency:
Add more mineral spirits to thin or whiting to thicken.
To darken the cement, add more lamp black.
The cement can be used immediately or stored if covered with a lid.

Design

Consider the final positioning of the glass panel and its surroundings. An old house, for example, with original features and antique furniture, might suggest a more traditional approach than a modern house where a contemporary design might be more appropriate. The main point to remember when designing a stained glass project is to keep it simple. The overall panel should be made up of simple component shapes bearing in mind the lead or copper foil as an integral part of the design. Don't make your job overly difficult by using shapes that are virtually impossible to cut. Dividing up a complex shape into smaller sections often makes cutting much easier.

When designing a window, it's a good idea to start by simply doodling on a piece of paper. Once you are satisfied with the general appearance, measure the opening and draw it to scale. Finalize the design on the small-scale sketch, making any alterations necessary, and then fill in the glass spaces with colored pencils to give yourself an idea of what the final effect will be. If you make a few photocopies of the sketch first, you will be able to try several different color combinations so that you can compare the effect of each. Alternatively, you could outline the lead lines on the sketch with India ink and fill in the spaces with water colors to get a better representation of the completed piece.

Once you are satisfied with the design, pin it up where you can look at it often over the next few days — it's far easier to alter the drawing than it is to change the glass panel after you have finished and installed it. When you are completely satisfied with the design, you should make up a cartoon (cartoon is the traditional name for the full-size drawing).

Drawing the Cartoon

Use white paper for the cartoon unless you will be working on a light box, in which case use tracing paper. The light box is used mainly when a design employs a lot of dark or translucent glass. It makes it easier to see the line of the cartoon when you are cutting the glass panes. If the design is very simple, it should be possible to draw it freehand up to full-size by referring to your smaller sketch. However, most designs are complex enough to warrant using a grid to enlarge the design. Some of the designs in this book are actual size but if you should choose one that needs enlarging, it can be done quite successfully in this way.

Copper Foil or Lead Came

It is important to be aware of the jointing material you are going to use as this affects the thickness of the outline drawn on the cartoon. If you have not already chosen the method of construction, now is the time to decide whether to use lead came or copper foil. If you do not know which method to use, then consider the following guidelines.

Copper foil lends itself to three-dimensional projects, small pieces, delicate objects, and indoor applications. Lead is preferable for outdoor use, larger pieces and strong bold designs. Three-dimensional work in lead is possible but it tends to look heavy and somewhat cumbersome.

If you are using copper foil, use a thin pencil line, $\frac{1}{32}$ inch (.75mm), to draw the outline of the glass pieces. If you are using lead came, you will need to draw a thicker line, $\frac{1}{16}$ inch (1.5mm), to represent the space taken up by the heart of the came itself. A felt-tipped pen is ideal for this purpose. If you do not enlarge the lines when you are drawing out the cartoon, then the cut glass will not fit together accurately and the overall size of the panel will expand significantly.

Using a Light Box or Making a Pattern

Once you have produced the full-size cartoon, you are then faced with two methods of cutting the glass to shape. The simplest method is to place the glass directly on the illuminated cartoon and cut to the line seen through the glass. This method is only useful for glass you can see through. For very light types of glass, the light box is unnecessary.

Making a pattern is applicable to all types of glass especially opalescent, mirror, and dark glass. To make the actual pattern, lay some thin white cardboard on a flat surface and place a piece of carbon paper face-down onto it. Cover the carbon paper with the cartoon and pin the papers together to stop them from shifting during the copying process. Carefully and firmly trace all the lines on the cartoon using a sharp pencil. You'll find it easier

ENLARGING THE DESIGN

Divide the design into a number of squares — the more complex the design, the smaller the squares. Now divide the full size paper into a similar number of larger squares. Then use this grid as reference to redraw each line in the small box into the corresponding large box. With a little patience you will be able to transfer the design accurately creating the full scale cartoon. An easy method of reduction is to take measurements for the panel in inches and convert them into centimeters (eg. 12 inches becomes 12cm). See below.

TECHNIQUES

to see which lines you have already done if you use a colored pencil. While the sheets are still pinned together, number each piece. This is extremely important as the next stage is to separate the sheets and cut the cardboard pattern into individual pieces. If you are using lead came, go over the lines with the thick pen to compensate for the thickness of the heart of the came. It is also useful to mark each piece for color, as this will enable you to estimate quite accurately how much glass of each type and color you will need. Simply group all pieces of each color and measure out the area of glass you require.

Cutting the Pattern

For copper foil work it is sufficient to cut down the center of the thin line but for lead work it is essential to cut away the thickness of the line to account for the heart of the lead. Special shears are available for this purpose, but they are unnecessary unless you plan to do a great deal of work with lead came. A good substitute can be made by taping together two single edged razor blades with a $\frac{1}{16}$ inch (1.5mm) wooden or cardboard spacer in between.

Selecting the Glass

Most color in everyday life is seen as reflected light but the color in stained glass is unusual in that it is filtered light. Depending on the light source, the color in glass can vary in intensity, appearing quite different under different circumstances. This effect is one of the great attractions of stained glass as an artistic medium.

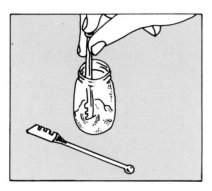

The cutter should be kept in a jar containing a layer of cloth soaked in a mixture of one part household oil and two parts mineral spirits. Between every two or three cuts dip the cutter in the jar to keep it clean and lubricated, which will prolong the life of the cutter. Replace the cutter when it becomes blunt.

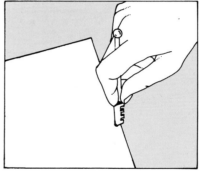

Start by placing the cutter between the first and second fingers of your writing hand. Close your thumb and first finger on to the grip of the cutter. Tuck the remaining fingers in towards the palm. Hold the cutter perpendicular to the glass at the edge nearest to you with the wheel forward and the notches towards you. You should stand while cutting and the bench should be just below waist height.

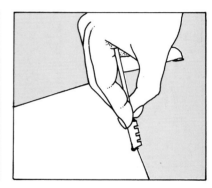

There are alternative methods of holding the cutter that will help to give the extra downward pressure necessary to produce a good score. Hold the cutter, notches upwards, in the palm of your hand and parallel to the fingers. Close the thumb on to the shaft of the cutter and rotate the wrist so that the cutter is perpendicular to the glass. Tuck the last two fingers in towards the palm.

When choosing glass, bear in mind the amount of available light in the panel's final position. Do not choose really dark glass for internal locations because their effect will be lost without adequate back-lighting.

In terms of color, individual choice varies, however there are a few things to keep in mind. Blue and red side by side for example, will produce a mauve haze, creating an almost blurred image. If this effect is not desired, small areas of white or clear glass can be introduced between them. This principle was often used in the twelfth and thirteenth centuries when blues and reds were used extensively. Yellow set beside red and blue will create a very strong effect that could overwhelm a design and make it appear gaudy.

When you are working with oranges, purples, and greens, you may wish to intersperse lighter tints to soften the overall effect and pull forward the main elements in the design. Although color is a very important feature that can change the whole atmosphere of a particular space, a common fault, especially with beginners, is the use of too much color. You will achieve a far more pleasing effect by using strong bold color in small areas, perhaps for a central motif, and leaving the softer lighter colors to provide the background. This will result in a composition with a natural focus. As you work, be prepared to be a little flexible. You may find that alternative colors work better in certain positions. If possible, keep a range of colors near the cutting bench to allow yourself the opportunity to make last

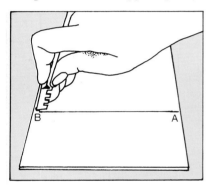

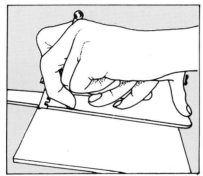

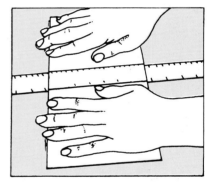

Ensure that the bench is flat and the glass is supported evenly. Gently place the cutter on the edge of the glass nearest you. Apply a downward pressure and push the cutter forward from point A to point B keeping the downward pressure constant. Listen for the glass "singing" as the cutter travels across the glass. Continue until you get to within ⅛ inch (3mm) from the opposite edge and lift the cutter. This will prevent you chipping the glass. The score should be clearly visible and continuous. Remember — do not go over the same score twice as this will blunt the cutter and reduce the chance of a clean break.

Put the straight edge on the glass and hold it firmly in place. Place the cutter on the opposite edge of the glass and line up the face of the cutter with the straight-edge. Apply the usual downward pressure necessary to effect a score and a slight sidewards pressure against the guiding edge. Pull the cutter towards you. The result will be a perfectly straight line. The score line should begin and end ⅛ inch (3mm) from each edge.

Having checked the score, place the glass on a ruler with the score uppermost centered along the edge of the ruler. Place the palm of one hand on one side of the score and push the glass to the bench. Place the palm of the other hand on the opposite side and slowly apply pressure on the glass until it snaps. This method is very safe and ideally suited to large panes.

minute changes when you feel inspired.

Cutting the Glass

Once you have selected the glass, place the first color over the corresponding outline on the cartoon. Place the cartoon on a light box if necessary. Arrange the outlines so that there is minimum wastage. You will need to leave at least ¼ inch (6mm) all the way round the shape to trim off, otherwise the cut edge will tend to break away in small pieces leaving a rough finish. Alternatively place a pattern piece on top of the glass and draw around it with a pen that marks on glass. The thinner the line drawn by this pen, the more accurate the cut will be. When you are cutting the glass, use the inside of the pen line as your guide. Again, when laying out the pieces, leave at least ¼ inch (6mm) to trim off. If you only have large pieces of glass to start with, cut off a strip in a width that will be useful to you and then subdivide it into shorter lengths.

Glass is a particularly hard material that, by its very nature, can only be cut by a material that is harder than itself. Unlike wood, glass has no grain — all the atoms are arranged irregularly, therefore the tension is fairly uniform throughout. The function of the cutter is to effect a score in the glass surface, thereby producing a line of weakness. When the glass is put under pressure along the score line, this weakness develops into a crack that eventually runs the length of the glass and separates it. It is important to separate the glass soon after it has been scored because of the structural changes

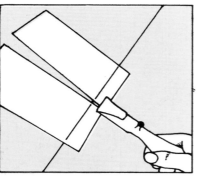

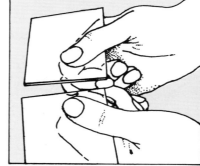

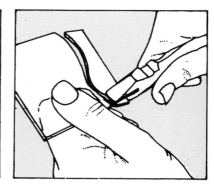

Place the glass 2 inches (50mm) over the edge of the bench with the score uppermost. Place the jaws of the pliers directly over the score with the concave jaw on top. If the pliers have an adjustment screw, set the jaws to lightly grip the glass then unscrew half a turn. Squeeze the jaws gently together. The glass will first crack at the end nearest you and run all the way along the score to the other end. These pliers are designed for straight cuts but can be used for very slight curves.

This method is most suitable for medium size pieces of glass, straight cuts, and slight curves only. Make your hands into fists and hold the glass with thumbs on top and fingers underneath, score side uppermost. Line the score up with the join between your two index fingers. Grip the glass firmly and roll your knuckles apart.

Breaking pliers are used to grip small pieces of glass that cannot be broken out by hand. Hold the bulk of the glass in one hand and place the pliers almost on top of the score at the edge of the glass. Grip the glass firmly with your hand and the pliers and break the score downwards. This method is especially useful for curved cuts.

that take place within the glass after scoring.

You should never go over the same score twice. It will damage the cutting wheel and it will not have any effect on the glass except to make it less likely to break cleanly. Traditionally, a diamond was used to score the glass but today a steel or tungsten carbide wheel is used in stained glass work because it is more effective for producing curved lines.

You may feel that cutting glass is a very difficult process, but by following the instructions carefully and observing closely the effects of what you are doing at each stage, you will soon develop the skill required to produce perfect results. Practice on scraps of glass first and get acquainted with the tools and materials before working on more expensive glass.

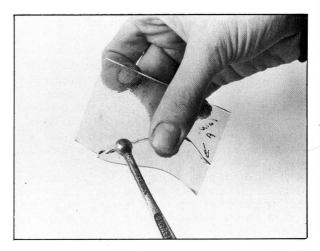

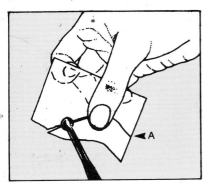

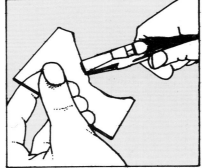

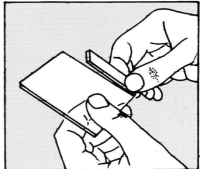

This method is suitable for all sizes of glass and all types of cuts, straight and curved. It is used mainly in conjunction with and to assist other breaking methods. Used by itself it leaves an uneven edge that is often quite sharp. Start by lightly tapping the glass with the ball end of your cutter. Aim the blows to strike the glass directly on the score line but on the reverse side of the glass. Between each tap check to see if a crack has appeared. When it does, tap the glass further along the score until the glass separates. Hold both sides of the glass so that they do not fall uncontrollably. Tapping the glass to produce a crack first will greatly assist in the other breaking methods.

Glass can be gently nibbled away to clean up uneven edges by using grozing pliers. Hold the bulk of the glass in one hand, or if it is a large piece, set it slightly over the end of the bench. With the pliers grip the glass lightly, covering only 1/16 inch (1.5mm) at a time. Slowly increase the biting pressure of the jaws and roll the pliers down at the same time. Repeat this procedure until all the excess is removed. This process does not square up the edge entirely but it will save you cutting a whole new piece.

Glass is sharp and should be handled with a reasonable amount of care. The biggest fear is cutting yourself. To avoid this, dull the edges of your cut by scraping the edge with a piece of scrap glass at right angles or use a carborundum stone. This is especially important when working with copper foil as the sharp points can pierce the foil. Throw small pieces of glass in a scrap box while you are cutting. Also keep a table brush handy and sweep off your work bench to remove small chips and slivers. Sweep into a box.

You will also find that cutting glass is easier when you understand its properties and limitations. Start by obtaining some clear glass $1/16$-$1/8$ inch (2-3mm) thick, about 8 inch (20cm) square, some tracing paper and trace the lines illustrated on this page. Start with the straight line A and progress through to Line D following the instructions given in the step by step diagrams on the next pages.

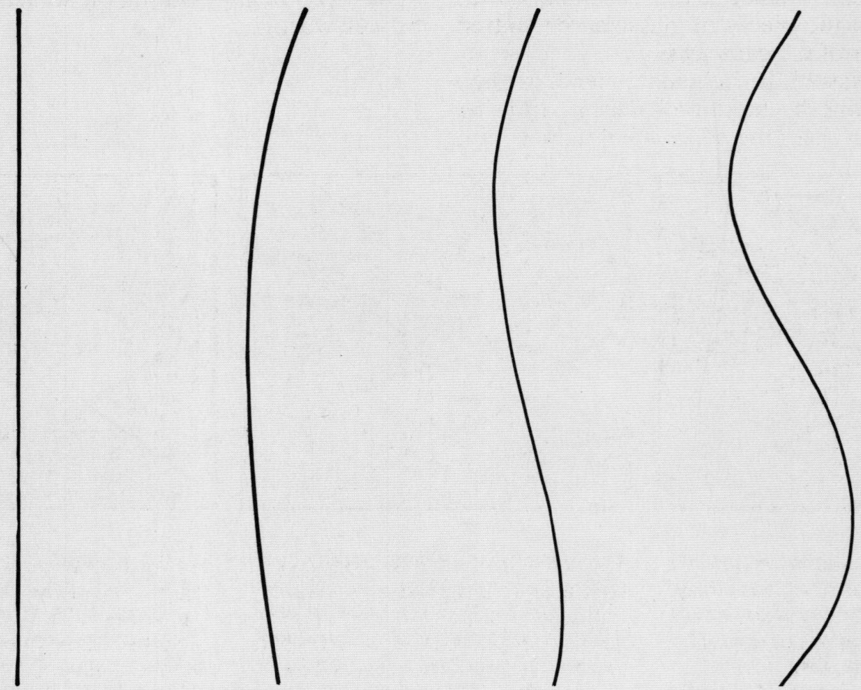

Cutting to a pattern:

The key word here is accuracy. No matter how few pieces of glass you intend to assemble, each piece must be cut with precision. It is simply not enough to be able to cut glass roughly to shape and hope for the best. Take your time while scoring the glass. If you wish you can stop the cutter halfway along a score as long as you keep the downward pressure constant. This will enable to review the outline before you make a detour. When cutting glass to a copper foil outline, get the wheel to travel down the center of the thin line. When cutting for the lead, make sure you use the thick line for its intended purpose, cut the left hand piece of glass to the left edge of the line and the right hand piece of glass to the right hand edge of the line. Think of it as two lines.

It is best to cut all the glass of one color at one time starting with the largest piece. Once cut, check it against the cartoon or pattern piece. If it is satisfactory, then mark the cartoon or place the pattern to one side so that it is not cut it again.

Arrange the cut glass either on a copy of the cartoon or, if space is limited, in piles of one color.

Once all the pieces of glass are cut, you can begin the leading or foiling processes. Here you will see the importance of the building board. Before you can use the lead, it must be stretched to straighten it and remove any kinks or twists that have resulted from handling. This is done by gripping one end of the strip in the jaws of a vice while holding the other end with pliers and pulling back firmly and evenly. This procedure will add approximately 3 inch (75mm) to a 6 feet (1.8m) length of lead came. Once the came has been stretched, it must be opened with a lathkin so that the pieces of glass can be slotted into the channels of the came easily.

Foiling the edges of the individual pieces of glass can either be done by hand or by using a foiling machine. In both cases the edges are wrapped with the adhesive backed foil strip and the overlap is folded over the face of the glass.

The strips of copper foil or pieces of lead came around each piece of glass are joined together with solder. The control of the heat is critical in order for the jointing to be successful. Too much heat and the lead will melt, too little and the solder will not flow freely. Proper preparation of the joints themselves is also important if you want to achieve perfect results. Time spent practicing with a soldering iron before you begin working on an actual project will be well worth it.

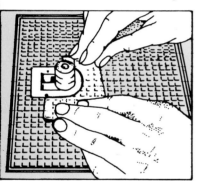 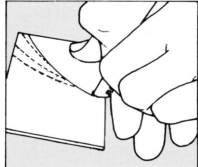 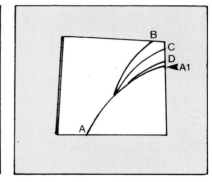

Grinders can be used to smooth the cut edges of a piece of glass. They are useful in that they can tidy up bad cutting and take off sharp edges. Carefully mark the glass to be ground, work to the lines. Offer the glass to the grinding wheel and apply light pressure only. Always wear safety goggles when you are grinding glass. The wheel of the grinder is kept moist all times to prolong its life, so be sure you are holding the glass securely as it can be slippery.

The same method of scoring straight lines applies to curved lines. You will find using your other hand to guide your cutting hand useful. Some cuts will be concave and some will be convex. The method of breaking the glass is different for each. In both cases a series of scores is necessary.

Convex curves are simpler to separate than concave ones. Follow the diagram. Start at Point A and push the cutter to Point A1. Next, turn the glass around so that Point B is nearest you. Cut from Point B to B1 taking care not to continue along the first score. Proceed from Point C to Point C1 and finally D to D1. You now have a series of fairly straight scores that, when broken individually, will result in a cut, A-A1, being produced.

TECHNIQUES

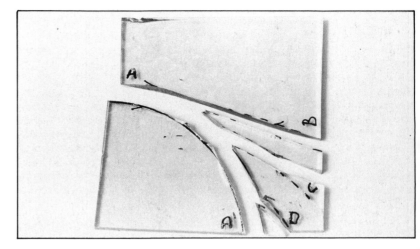

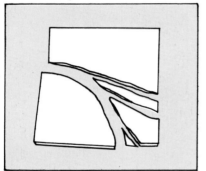

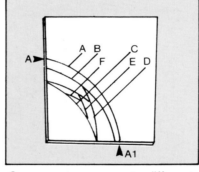

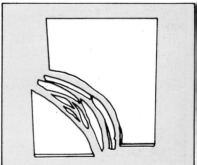

It is important to break the scores in the right order. Start with Point B and break this score by hand or pliers. The glass will separate from Point B· to A. Next proceed to Point C and break the score to Point B1. Follow on with Point D to C1 and D1. The number of extra cuts depends on the length and steepness of the curve.

Concave curves present a different set of rules. This time the glass has to be broken out progressively to avoid losing the tails. Start at Point A and continue to A1 then from Point B to B1 and C to C1.

Break the score C-C1 away. Next score the lines D-E-F-G. You now have a series of short curves that are broken out in the following order with pliers: Points G-F-E-D-B and A. The number of extra cuts will depend on the steepness and length of the curve. Always cut the concave curves of a shape first, as they are more difficult to cut and may take several attempts.

TROUBLE SHOOTING

Symptom
Glass not breaking:

1. Score is not deep enough	Check the wheel for wear. Increase cutting pressure.
2. Score too deep	Reduce cutting pressure.
3. Fulcrum/pressure incorrect	Check that the score is above the fulcrum and uppermost on the surface of the glass. Check if hands are incorrectly placed beside score line.

Glass breaking incorrectly:

1. Cutting wheel damaged producing dotted line	Change wheel or cutter
2. Uneven downward pressure while scoring	Practice scoring on scrap glass.
3. Previous scratch/score in glass	Select new glass
4. Uneven stress in glass (particularly hand blown glass)	This can be difficult as uneven stress is not usually apparent. Try tapping
5. Curve too acute	Make extra cuts as described
6. Fulcrum uneven, or grit between fulcrum and glass	Ensure bench surface is perfectly flat. Ensure fulcrum is also flat and straight. Clean work surface and fulcrum.
7. Score left too long	Start afresh.
8. Tapping glass was too violent	Produce lighter taps.
9. Cutter lifted off too soon or cutter lifted and replaced on or near the score	Once a score has started, you must continue to the edge of the glass.

If you encounter any of the above problems it is probably better to start afresh.

General Notes and Tips

Never wipe the cutting bench clean with the hand; use a brush. Keep some adhesive bandages handy and always wash and cover cuts.
Use protective goggles whenever possible.
Use gloves when handling large sheets of glass above your head in case you slip or if the glass has an unseen crack it could fall apart.
When cutting glass, try to be relaxed.
Run the edges of newly cut glass against each other (as if sharpening a knife) as this will take the sharp edges off, especially inner curves.
Glass always breaks out from the score (see diagram).
Keep all sizeable pieces of scrap glass for future use.

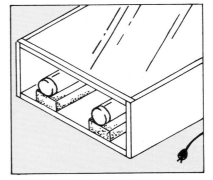

Making a light box
If you have selected some dark glass it will be easier to cut using a light box as the lines of the cartoon will then show clearly through the glass. Build a box 8 inches (20cm) deep. Length and width are determined by the size and number of fluorescent light tubes you select. Paint the inside of the box white. Attach two or more fluorescent tubes to the bottom approximately 6 inches (15cm) from the front and back and 6 inches apart. Drill holes in the sides of the box for ventilation. On top, place a piece of frosted glass, shiny side up. The wiring is not difficult.

TECHNIQUES

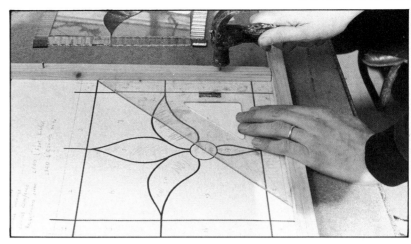

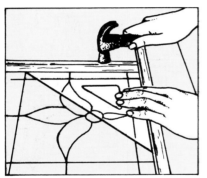

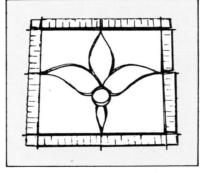

For both leading up and copper foil work, you will need a board at least 6 inches (150mm) bigger all round than the finished panel. Chipboard, not plywood, is the ideal material. Lay the full size cartoon on the board, positioning it in the center. Take a 2x1 inch (50x25mm) wooden batten and lay it along the longest edge of the drawing. Make sure that it is positioned exactly on the edge of the line to ensure that the glass will be positioned correctly. Take a second batten and place it at a 90° angle to the first batten. If you are right handed it should be on the left hand side of the drawing. Use a set square to ensure it is positioned accurately.

Lay all your pieces of glass against the pattern and check they are all cut accurately. Having done this, remove them one at a time and lay them out ready for the next stage. If you have a copy of the full size cartoon, you can lay them on this.

Select a length of lead suitable for the perimeter of the panel. Take into consideration the width of the rebate in the wooden frame. Allow ⅛ inch (3mm) extra to enable the lead frame to be visible inside the wooden frame. To make the lead ready for use, all the kinks and twists have to be taken out. Place one end of the lead in the lead vice and untwist its entire length. Grip the other end of the lead with a pair of household pliers. Take up the tension and slowly pull out the lead. The lead will straighten out and actually stretch a few inches. Stand with one foot behind the other to balance yourself in case the lead snaps.

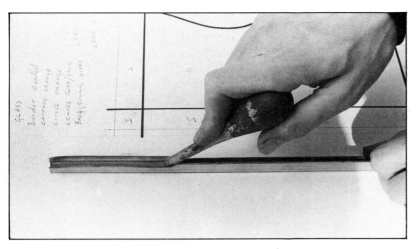

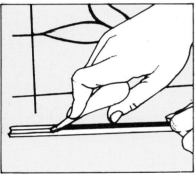

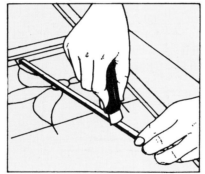

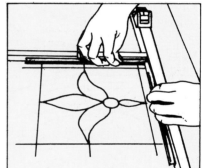

Open up the channels of the lead to accommodate the glass with a tool called a lathkin. A lathkin is simply a piece of hard wood that is wedge-shaped and runs along the channel of the lead opening the leaf. Lay the came so that the section is the same way up as the letter H. Alternatively lay the lead on its side and against a strip of wood for support. Both methods are quite successful. Keep the lathkin oiled or waxed to assist its progress. Draw or push the lathkin along the length of the lead.

There are two common ways to cut lead, either with a lead knife or with cutting pliers. The action of the knife is to gently rock the blade through the lead rather than sawing or slicing, which might crush the lead. Keep the blade upright and always cut on a firm surface with a sharp blade. Some joints will have to be mitered at various angles to suit the glass at hand. Having cut the joint, open up the leaves, if necessary using the end of the knife. Never use a razor, scalpel, carpenter's knife, and so on, to cut the lead as the blade could snap and do you some harm. When using pliers, simply place the jaws over the lead at the required length and angle and gently squeeze.

The first two border leads should be at least 1 inch (25mm) longer than the drawing. Place the largest lead against the drawing and the battens so the end butts up to the adjacent side. With the lead knife, open up the top inside leaf at the corner and insert the next lead.

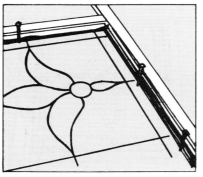

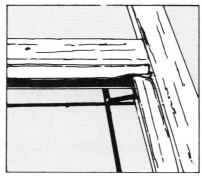

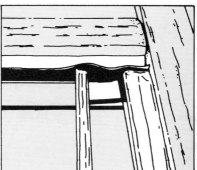

The leads and glass are held in place before soldering by glazing or horseshoe nails, positioned alongside the components at strategic points. The exact position of the nails for each panel will be different. Glazing nails are shaped specifically for ease of manual extraction. Do not use excessive force to bang them in. If you do not have glazing nails, you can substitute 2 inch (50mm) ovals. Start by placing a nail against the edge of each free end of the two leads.

Take the corner piece of the glass and slide it into position in the leads. Lift the glass slightly to ensure a sound fit. Gently tap the glass into position using a wooden block or the weighted handle of the lead knife. Once in position, check the cartoon against the edge of the glass and make any adjustments necessary. Assess the position of the battens against the cartoon before trimming the glass.

When the piece is positioned correctly, take a stretched-out piece of lead of the right width, and cut it to a convenient length. Offer the lead to the glass and butt the end up to the perimeter lead. Open the perimeter lead to accommodate this new lead and insert it. Mark the end of the lead to be trimmed. The actual position of this mark is dependent on the width of the lead that will be butted up to it. This distance has to be judged, however in all cases, the lead is slightly shorter than the length of glass.

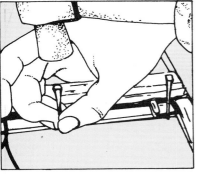
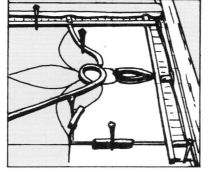

Once you have marked the lead, remove it and cut to length. If the joint is mitered, the mark should take this into account. Replace the cut lead to its original position and check its accuracy. Insert a glazing nail on the outer edge of the glass, being careful not to place it too tightly which could chip the glass. Surround the nail with your hand so that if the hammer slips off the nail your hand will prevent the hammer from smashing the glass.

Take the next piece of glass and repeat the procedure. Glass and leads are positioned in a logical sequence that will vary from project to project. Place the next pane of glass so that it gives maximum support to the last and provides a good base for the next. To avoid chipping the pieces of glass, you can place a ½ inch (12mm) length of lead against the glass first and nail to that. Some people tuck every internal lead into the next and others simply butt the leads together. As long as the joints actually meet and there is no gap, you will have no problems.

When all the pieces of glass are in position, the last two leads are laid and perimeter leads trimmed. To ensure the squareness of the panel lay battens up against the exposed edges and nail them into position.

TROUBLE SHOOTING LEAD WORK
1. First few pieces of glass incorrectly placed
2. Glass at a later stage not positioned correctly

Suspect the battens are out of alignment. Adjust the cartoon. There are several remedies for this. Make sure the glass is seated in the leads and the adjoining leads are seated on the previous glass. Trim off excess. This might not be on the side that is protruding so start by marking the glass while in position on the edges where the glass meets the lead. Use a felt-tipped pen and run it around the leaf of the lead, remove the glass and note if the line is parallel to the edge of the glass. If

it is, then trim the edge that is not conforming to the cartoon. If all this fails cut a new piece from a template as follows. Take a scrap of clear glass and place it over the faulty shape — preferably while it is still in place, as this will hold the leads in their correct position. With a thin pen draw around the shape, using the lead as a guide. You have to judge where the heart of the lead starts. Cut the template and check for fit. If this is correct use the new piece as a pattern to cut the replacement glass.

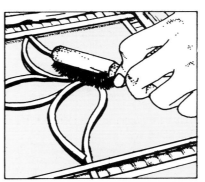

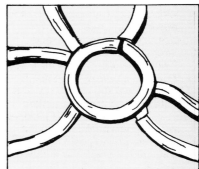

Before you actually start soldering, the joints have to be cleaned and fluxed ready to accept solder. Using a wire brush, rub over all the joints until the lead oxide is removed. All joints will appear bright silver. It is possible to use medium grade steel wool but this sometimes leaves deposits behind that interfere with the soldering.

Now and again leads will seem to shrink mysteriously and what was once butted will separate. This is the result of slight shifting of the glass and lead as you work across the panel. To compensate for this, small slivers of matching lead are inserted. Cut the length necessary to fill the gaps. Lay it on its side and cut down the heart to give you a "T" section. Place the tail of the "T" in the hole to fill the gap. This will need to be done again on the reverse side once the panel is turned over.

LEADING TIPS

CUTTING ACUTE ANGLES IN LEAD

Sometimes, the angle to be cut is so acute that the lead knife tends to crush the heart and the leaves fold right over. Place a nail in the bench and then butt the came, channel side up, on to the nail. Following the mark cut the lead at an acute angle with the lead knife. Hold the lead knife at the correct angle and cut towards the nail.

Now and again the lead gets so mangled up even when it has been stretched that the leaves are folded so tight you cannot use the lathkin to separate them. Try inserting your lead knife and carefully prying them open. Follow on with the lathkin. Then, if the leaves are cockled due to the action of the knife, draw the knife at an acute angle to flatten them down again not as far closed as they were before but to the usual unopened position. Then open them up again with the lathkin.

Store the leads in a long box, wrapped in paper or polythene, as this will keep them in good order. Try not to buy lead rolled into a coil. Keep your leftover leads in a smaller box for future. Collected scrap lead is money.

LEADING A CIRCULAR WINDOW
Method 1

Use the 90° jig and cut a piece of glass as illustrated with an inner curve corresponding to the circumference of the window. Place this glass in the jig and lay your first lead to this. Choose a suitably easy section to start the internal leading as many nails may be needed to hold the first few bits of glass in place.

LEADING A CIRCULAR WINDOW
Method 2

Place a series of nails around the perimeter of the pattern and bed a lead to give the circumference.

TRIANGULAR AND STRAIGHT SIDED WINDOWS

Set the jig at the required angle.

ARCHED AND SCALLOPED TOP WINDOWS

Make two templates, one for the shape of the window frame and one concave for the shape of the parameter concerned. Continue assembly until you reach the curved edge. Lay the last lead in place and insert the template. Batten down as usual. Check the overall size and shape by using the window frame template.

TECHNIQUES

The soldering iron is used to heat the solder that is applied to each joint. When cool the solder sets hard and sticks the leads together. There are many types of solder, the most suitable for lead being a mixture of tin and lead — 60 percent tin and 40 percent lead. This is because its melting temperature is less than the melting point of the lead came.

What is flux? Flux is an agent applied to metals before they are soldered to assist in the flow of the solder. However, this flux is corrosive and will slowly eat away the tip of your iron. All soldering should be done in a well-ventilated room and ideally a fan should be used to blow away the fumes before you inhale them.

There are several types of flux for lead work. The most common is oleic acid in liquid or paste form. This is corrosive. It works well and reduces the amount of abrasion needed to clean the joint as it also has a cleansing action. A resin flux is just as effective as an acid flux, yet being noncorrosive, it reduces the wear on the tip. However, you may find that it leaves a gummy residue.

Tinning the Iron

Tinning is a term used to describe coating a surface with (tin) solder. The tip of the iron must be tinned before use as it will be useless otherwise. Make sure, before you plug in a new iron, that you know whether it is tinned or not. Instructions are given below for this process.

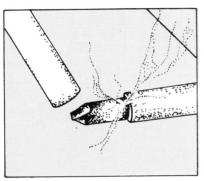 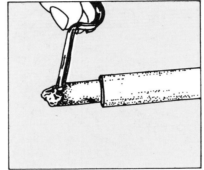

While the soldering iron is still cold, cover the tip with flux. Turn the iron on and let it heat up, and wait until the flux begins to smolder.

Hold the iron against some solder and keep the solder moving around its surface. As soon as the solder starts to melt, quickly switch the iron off and apply solder to the entire surface, fluxing liberally. Do this over the bench as you are likely to drip hot solder. Once the iron is completely tinned, switch it back on, and allow it to heat up. Wipe off any excess solder from the tip of the iron with a damp sponge. It's best to keep the sponge on the bench and present the iron to it. If the solder did not take the iron and it has a copper tip, file it down to the bare metal and repeat the procedure. If the tip is iron clad, allow it to cool. Gently clean the tip with fine grade steel wool. If the tip is old, check to see if the cladding is still intact. Signs to look for are a surface that is worn and pitted, or cladding that is bubbling and separating from the base. If either of these conditions occur, you must replace the tip of the iron.

SOLDERING TIPS

1. ALWAYS rest the iron on a suitable stand — brick is excellent.
2. NEVER leave an iron unattended — it could cause a fire or hurt an unsuspecting person.
3. ALWAYS, even when cold, hold the iron by the handle — it is good practice.
4. NEVER let the iron overheat — either use it, as this will take the heat away, or switch it off.
5. ALWAYS keep the iron tinned and clean — use a wet sponge while soldering.
6. NEVER file an iron-clad (long-life) tip — you will ruin it.
7. ALWAYS use an iron of the right caliber for the job — see Tools Chapter.
8. NEVER use an iron as a hammer, screwdriver, or saw — you will damage it.

Good & Bad solder joints

A good joint should be small and smooth. It should join the leads securely and be almost invisible. Bad joints tend to be large and bumpy or do not actually join the leads. The usual reasons for a bad joint are a cool iron, too much or too little solder or incorrect application. A soldering iron is not a paint brush. Its motion should be confined to up and down and only on long joints should it move laterally. The soldering bench should also be level or the liquid solder will run downhill. Having soldered all joints, clean off the flux residue with the wire brush.

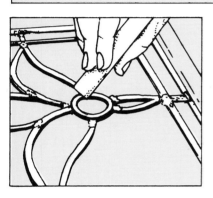 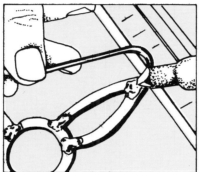

Brush all the joints liberally with flux to prepare them for soldering. Test the iron to ensure it is not hot enough to melt the leads. If it is, unplug for several minutes.

Place the solder stick on the joint and apply heat to the solder. The iron should melt the solder within 23 seconds and no force should be employed to speed up this melting process. Once the solder is melted, the iron should be left on the joint just long enough for the solder to transfer to the lead as too much heat will burn the lead away. Once the solder transfers to the lead, lift the iron vertically off the joint. The whole process should only take 5-6

seconds. If the lead is not joined, allow it to cool and come back to it. If you have burned a hole in the lead it will need to be filled, as outlined previously. Some joints, because of their length, require you to draw the solder along the entire seam. Start at one end feeding solder as you travel. Lifting the iron off the other end to produce an even seam.

TECHNIQUES

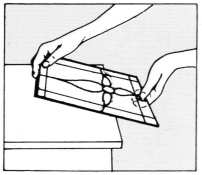

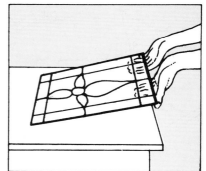

Most small panels are easily turned but larger ones need to be supported to prevent them from bending. Slide the panel over the edge of the bench until it reaches the point of balance. Drop the edge nearest you while lifting the opposite edge with your other hand. At the same time allow the panel to slide further against the bench. Keep the panel against the bench until it is vertical.

Lift the panel on to the bench or, if it is easier, down to the floor. Turn the panel about-face keeping it vertical at all times. Reverse the procedure to set the panel back on the bench. If the panel is really big, slide it off the bench straight on to a piece of board, which will give it all-over support. You may require assistance for this procedure.

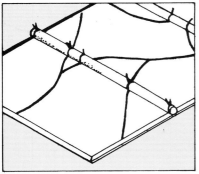

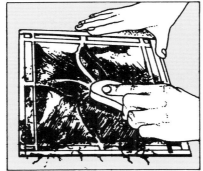

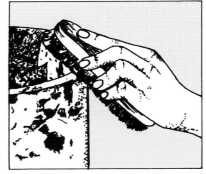

If the glass panel is larger than four square feet, it may be necessary to attach a steel or brass bar across the back. The bar or bars are placed approximately every 20 inches (49cm) of window length. This prevents the window from sagging. Solder copper wire lengths to each inside lead joint the bar passes and over the two border leads. Attach the bar by placing it over the wires and twist them tightly around the bar. Solder the wires.

Once you have soldered both sides of the panel it must be made watertight. Putty or putty-cement is forced between the leads and the glass with a stiff brush. This is a messy process so transfer the panel on to a board that will be used for nothing but cementing or cover your glazing board with newspapers. Take a scrubbing brush and load it with cement from the tub. Apply the cement to the panel with a circular motion, ensuring that all the leads have been filled.

Clean the brush of excess cement by drawing the brush across the top of the cement tub so the cement is not wasted. With the empty brush, start scrubbing the panel again. This will begin to lift the excess cement off the panel. Keep the brush as clean as possible. Fill and clean both sides of the panel.

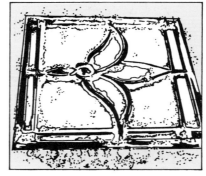

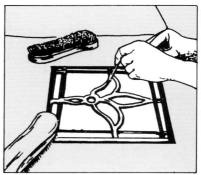

Close the outside leaves of the perimeter leads together with the lathkin or similar tool. Run the tool along the leaf several times rather than applying too much pressure at one time. Repeat the process on the inside of the panel. Any excess cement will ooze out and should be brushed off. If the internal leads are a flat profile, they can be flattened as well. Clean off all the excess cement with the stiff brush and put it back in the tub.

Liberal amounts of whiting lightly brushed over both sides of the panel will absorb all the residual moisture from the cement. When it is semidry after about 4-5 hours remove the excess whiting with a soft brush.

Take a clean scrubbing brush and vigorously scrub the panel clean. Go around each shape with a blunt stick and pick it off any deposits of cement left on the glass. Continue brushing the panel until it is completely clean. Leave the panel to dry for a day or two before installation.

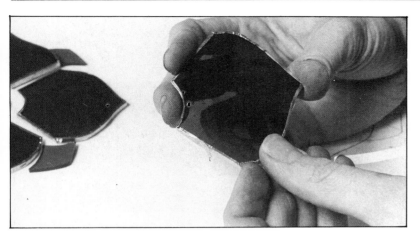

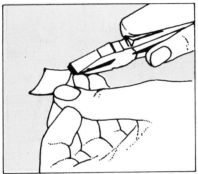

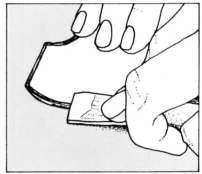

Take the first piece of glass and check the edges for sharp areas. If you find any, polish them off with a grinder. If you do not have one, then rub the irregularities away with the edge of another piece of glass or a fine carborundum stone. If the piece of glass has sharp points, nibble the tip off with the grozing pliers.

Peel two inches of the backing paper off the foil and position the adhesive area centrally on the edge of the glass. Hold the glass in a position so you can see down both sides at once. Once the foil is positioned, fold the edges down on to the surface of the glass. Make sure that the foil is firmly anchored to the glass. Peel off a further 2 inches, (5 cm) of backing and continue in this fashion until the glass is completely wrapped. Cut the end of the foil to allow ¼ inch (6mm) overlap. This joint should be positioned on the glass where it will be later hidden from view, as opposed to an outside edge. Continue this process for all the glass pieces.

Work around the foiled glass with a flat blunt stick making sure the foil is flattened onto the surface of the glass. Hold the stick at an acute angle and draw it towards yourself. When all the copper foil has been fixed, position all the pieces on the cartoon. Use a batten if necessary to secure the exposed edges making sure the panel is square.

Start by placing the solder at one end of the seam. Set the hot iron on the solder until it melts. As soon as it melts, feed more solder to the iron and draw the iron along the length of the seam. Try to feed the solder and move the iron at a speed to produce neither too much or too little molten solder. Most seams have to be built up in stages, especially if there are small gaps between the pieces of glass.

The glass may crack if subjected to prolonged heat, so the next layer is best left until the first layer has cooled. This will also prevent the

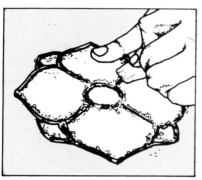

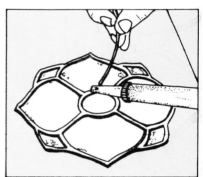

Plug in the soldering iron and allow it to warm up while you are fluxing the foil. With a brush apply flux on to all foil areas visible. If you are using a tallow candle, trace the foil along each piece of glass.

Once all fluxing is done test the soldering iron. When it is hot, start tacking the panel together at the points where three or more pieces join. The method of application is as follows. Place the solder stick on the joint and then place the iron on it. Leave the iron on the solder long enough for the solder to melt. Then remove the solder stick and lift the iron vertically away from the joint. Continue until all the pieces are tacked together.

solder will dropping through any gaps in the seam. Try to set the second layer down before the first layer melts.

The end result should be a neatly rounded bead, with all the joints running together. There should be no excess of solder spilling onto the surface of the glass and no valleys between the pieces. The only way to get the seam nicely rounded is to have the iron at the right temperature allowing the molten solder to float to its own level. The joints can be run together by allowing one second of extra heat at these points. This allows the adjacent cold seam to merge with the hot seam. Repeat the entire process on the other side of the panel.

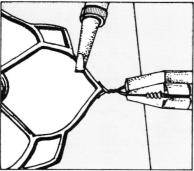

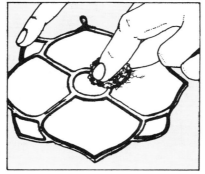

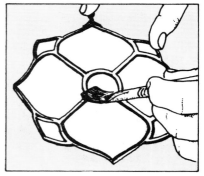

If you are making a light catcher or mobile, a loop must be soldered onto the finished article. This consists of a piece of copper wire that is twisted into a loop and the tails soldered to the appropriate place on the mobile. Having finished the soldering, the next step is to clean off all the flux residue once the panel has cooled. If the panel is small enough, immerse it in warm soapy water. If the panel is too big, sponge it with soapy water. A nail brush will help clean off the major dirt and the sponge will wipe it clean. Dry the workpiece with paper towels or a soft rag.

If you want to turn the seams of the solder another color by applying a patination agent, clean the solder further with some fine grade steel wool. Make sure you go over every seam on both sides and get into all the nooks and crannies. The seams may look clean after the first wash but they will probably have a thin film of soap that will resist the patination agent. Lightly brush off all the steel wool deposits from the workpiece. Patinas vary, so always read the manufacturers' instructions before proceeding. Always wear rubber gloves and keep clean water handy for washing yourself in a hurry, if necessary.

Apply the liquid to a small area with a rag or paint brush. If the effects do not start immediately, the solder is not clean enough. The solder should be turning bronze, copper, or black before your eyes. Generally speaking, the longer the agent is left on the seam the darker the effect. When the liquid dries, it can leave a crystalline precipitation on the glass that is very difficult to remove. Once the desired color is achieved, wash off in warm water and washing-up liquid. Patinas can be completely cleaned off with steel wool.

RENOVATION AND RESTORATION

The great revival of interest in period stained glass has made demands on the glass craftsman to restore old panels of glass that have fallen into serious disrepair as well as renovate panels that are in danger of becoming derelict. The first step in any renovation or restoration project is to assess the glass panel in terms of construction, design, and materials. Then the damage to the panel must be considered to determine the best approach for rectifying the problem. A small isolated area of damage, such as a cracked piece of glass, in an otherwise stable panel can often be taken care of with the panel in position. Needless to say this involves far less work and disruption than the removal of the entire panel from its position. However a major overhaul of a large panel will require many hours of work and often a temporary replacement must be fitted to the window or door opening while the work is being carried out.

Exterior door panels and windows can suffer a number of defects. The cause of damage to stained glass and leading are many. The results range from general deterioration of the lead and discoloration of the glass from sheer age, to mechanical damage due to climatic erosion or vandalism. Chemicals in the atmosphere can have a particularly devastating effect on very old panels of stained glass and when a panel has become seriously weakened because of erosion, it becomes extremely susceptible to damage from wind endangering the stability of the entire panel. However, fragile lead can be renewed and missing or damaged glass replaced with pieces matching the original in color, tone, and texture. If a panel is rare or very old and is in need of restoration it might be worth taking to a professional for advice rather than risking reducing its value by restoration at home.

Often panels of glass that at first appear to be in hopeless condition can be revived into beautiful examples of stained glass craftsmanship worthy of the effort required to restore them. Even if there are several pieces of broken or missing glass it is often possible to replace them with pieces cut from larger pieces of glass of a similar age and color to provide an almost perfect substitute. It is also possible to buy new glass in a wide variety of colors and finishes to make finding a suitable replacement easy.

If you are working on a symmetrical panel of glass in which one piece of glass has been broken you may find that you cannot get a suitable match to replace the broken piece. In this case, it may be worth replacing a couple of pieces to match up the pattern helping to make the new glass fit in to the overall design in an integrated way, leaving the repair less obvious. When you are looking for replacement glass always use color as your principle criteria because although texture does affect the look of the glass your eye will react to the color of the light more directly in the finished panel.

Sometimes the damage to glass panels is such that complete sections of the panel have been destroyed. In cases where this has happened and the panel is symmetrical it is possible to use the opposite side of the panel to produce a pattern for the missing area. However, if the design is irregular then you must rely on your own design skills to complete the missing section of the panel. It is often possible to use glass panels of the same period found in similar situations as your inspiration. Many books are available that contain period designs and time spent looking at period stained glass will certainly give you a sense of the way color and texture were used. Use anything you can for inspiration to help you create a new section that will be harmonious with the existing parts of the panel.

If you intend to reconstruct an entire panel using new lead take a careful look at the old came and try to match it as closely as possible for the most authentic restoration. Luckily the materials and techniques for stained glass work have changed very little over the past centuries and so accurate restoration is often fairly easy to achieve.

The most common form of damage is, not surprisingly, broken panes of glass, which, when confined to a single pane here and there, is not particularly serious. Extensive restoration is required when large areas of glass need replacing and perished lead has caused the panel to sag. If this is the case, then the panel will have to be stripped down entirely and rebuilt. Major repairs must be carried out in a logical sequence in order to ensure that the procedure goes smoothly and the panel is properly restored. Before you begin any repair

work, it's always a good idea to photograph the glass panel in its "before" state so you can use it as a reference while you are carrying out the repair. A photograph is always enjoyable to have to remind you of the state the glass panel was in before you rescued it.

Major repairs begin by taking the panel out of its framework and, if necessary, fitting a temporary replacement. The removal can be a very critical stage because often the stability of the panel has been seriously undermined and it is susceptible to even greater damage when it is being moved about unless extreme care is taken. Do not try to flatten out a distorted panel as that can cause cracking of the glass and a collapse of the entire panel. Accurate measurements should be taken of the panel in its framework so that you can be assured that the repaired panel will fit properly back into position. If the opening is irregular then it is a good idea to produce a template to ensure that the panel is rebuilt to the correct shape.

Once the panel has been removed from its framework it is laid on a workbench and a rubbing is taken of it to provide an accurate copy of the leadwork. A tracing is made of the rubbing from which a cartoon or working pattern is derived. The cartoon is notated with the color and type of glass in each position to make the reassembly easier. Other notation includes the thickness of the lead used on the original and the location of any tie bars or other reinforcement points. Once all the relevant information has been noted, then the panel is stripped down into its component parts.

Step-by-step the panel is dismantled and the old lead is discarded. The pieces of glass are taken and carefully laid over the cartoon in their corresponding position. This process begins at one side and methodically moves across the panel until the entire panel has been taken apart. Sections of broken glass can also be set aside as reference until replacements have been cut and fitted into position in the restored panel. The glass that is to be reused is cleaned, ready to be reassembled with the new pieces cut to replace broken sections.

The reassembly begins by choosing suitable replacement lead. Starting at one corner and working methodically across the panel the design is

reconstructed using new lead, the cleaned panes, and replacement glass where necessary. When all the pieces of the panel have been encased in lead, the joints are cleaned and sealed with solder on both the front and back of the panel.

The panel is sealed against the elements and given added rigidity by the putty based cement that is forced into the tiny gaps between the glass and the flanges of the lead came. Once the panel has been finally cleaned to remove any excess putty, it is ready to resume its place in its original framework.

Repairing copper foil work is similar to glazing individual panes of leaded glass. A pattern, with notes on the type and color of the damaged glass, is made by taking a rubbing. The broken pane is then

removed from the workpiece by carefully-aimed blows with a punch. A soldering iron is used to melt away the surrounding seam of solder and the copper foil is slowly pulled away using long-nosed pliers. The glass is cut to shape, wrapped with matching copper foil and inserted into place. The solder seam is built up again using exactly the same technique as new construction (see Chapter 3). Providing the glass is matched exactly, the restoration is truly invisible.

Once you have assessed the damage to the panel

of stained glass, accurate measurements should be taken of the panel in situ so that you can be sure of the repaired panel fitting exactly into position. If the shape of the panel is irregular then it is best to make a template of the opening to use as a guide when you are restoring the damaged panel. Clear glass makes a suitable template as you have all the materials and tools on hand and the glass can be re-used at a later date. However plywood or hardboard are also suitable for this purpose. It is possible to make a paper template but this is not as accurate as a solid version as it will be liable to distortion. Once a satisfactory record of the dimensions has been obtained, the window can be removed from the frame.

If the glass panel has been held in position by wooden strips nailed to the perimeter of the opening then this must be carefully removed so that it can be reused to secure the restored panel. Select the longest side and start in the center by driving a hacking knife between the frame and the bead. The knife is forced into the crack with sharp well-aimed blows from a medium weight hammer. Once the blade has been inserted, the beading is pried away from the frame inch by inch. If you hear a loud crack at this stage do not be too alarmed as it is usually the paint splitting or the nails squeaking through the bending of the wood strip away from the frame at the center; the overall length will be effectively reduced, allowing the mitered corners to part. Any

Starting anywhere on the perimeter hold the knife point at 90° to the surface of the putty and strike the back of the blade with a medium weight hammer. Force the point into the putty until it meets the wooden frame. Twist the blade until the putty cracks and a lump falls out. From this point work the knife into the rabbet and angle the blade so the next blow will hit the adjacent putty.

By working around the window, all putty can be removed from the face of the panel. Care must be taken to avoid further damage to the glass. If the hacking knife is not kept sharp, it is very easy to split the wooden frame by digging too deep. If this

happens, remove the knife at the same angle as it went in and continue hacking out in the opposite direction to avoid opening the split any further. If the putty is soft, it may be easier to remove using a shave hook, scraping it away bit by bit.

When moving a window unsupported make sure it is kept vertical, otherwise it will bend and glass could crack. If the window is bowed, do not push it flat against the supporting board as this might further damage the panel. Support the hollow by placing packing, such as crumpled-up old newspaper underneath it.

nails that are still embedded in the frame, stopping the beading from being removed can be either pulled out with pincers, or if they offer no purchase, bent over with a sharp blow from the knife and hammer. Once the first bead is removed, the adjoining two beads are then taken out. The last bead to be removed is the opposite the first. Next the window must be released from the putty bond.

Once all the putty has been removed from the frame, glazing nails or, more commonly, flat-headed tacks will be revealed at the corners, centers, and possible elsewhere around the window. These tacks will hold the panel in place while the putty sets need to be removed. Place the hacking knife under the head of the tack and lever against the frame. Protect the surface of the glass and use pliers to get a good grip on the nails to pull them out of the wooden frame.

Once the beading or putty and nails have been removed, the window is ready to come out. Invariably, however, the window has been embedded in putty that is inaccessable. By working the knife between the lead and wood and carefully prying the lead inch by inch towards the glass, the bond between lead and putty will be broken. By gently pushing the window from the outside it should be free enough to come out. Engage an assistant to ensure that it does not fall out.

When the window is free, allow it to tilt slightly inwards from the top and grip both sides. Keep the panel as near to vertical as possible at all times.

Lift the panel to the floor and lean it against a board, stout enough not to warp, with a batten nailed to the base to provide support. Rest the base of the panel on the batten, laying the panel against the board. In this way the window can be moved safely and effectively without further damage occurring.

Making a Pattern

To produce a balanced result, the pattern should be centered within the perimeter line. If the design is symmetrical then fold the tracing along the line of symmetry. Mark a thin pencil line on the fold and use this for measuring. If the design is unsymmetrical then the perimeter has to be lined up visually. By referring to your dimensions and the template, draw in the perimeter line. Remember the panel should be ⅛ inch (3mm) smaller all around than the size of the opening.

In the case of a severely damaged panel where portions of both glass and lead are missing, you will have to redesign the missing section. If the window is symmetrical you may already have the pattern. However, if this is not the case then a suitable infill will have to be drawn, based on reseach of similar designs.

Look carefully at the color and texture of the existing glass and try to identify the name of the glass and the method of production. If the original glass is no longer being made then suitable modern glass must be chosen to replace missing pieces. If the glass is hand made there is more chance of matching its characteristics compared to a sample of older machine-made glass. If the glass has a rolled textured surface then it may be possible that a very similar type of glass is still in production. Choose replacement glass for its color rather than the texture because the end result will be less noticeable. There is nothing worse than seeing a beautiful stained glass window ruined by incompatible glass substitutes.

Before the window can be stripped down a pattern has to be made. This is done by producing a rubbing, in much the same way that brass rubbings are taken. Lay the window on the bench, if necessary keep the window on the board. To stop the tracing paper from moving, pin it to the bench. Carefully run a wax block over the leads, making sure that all leads are marked. This rubbing is now an accurate record of the original pattern, however it is usually somewhat messy and does not provide enough detail to work from. Remove the rubbing from the window and lay flat.

Lay a fresh sheet of tracing paper over the top of the first rubbing. Go over all the leading lines with a black felt-tipped marker. Use a pen with a nib that produces a line ⅛ inch (3mm) wide to represent the heart of the lead came. Try to make this tracing as accurate as possible staying exactly in the center of the leading lines on the rubbing. This new line will represent the cutting line for any new pieces of glass.

RENOVATION AND RESTORATION

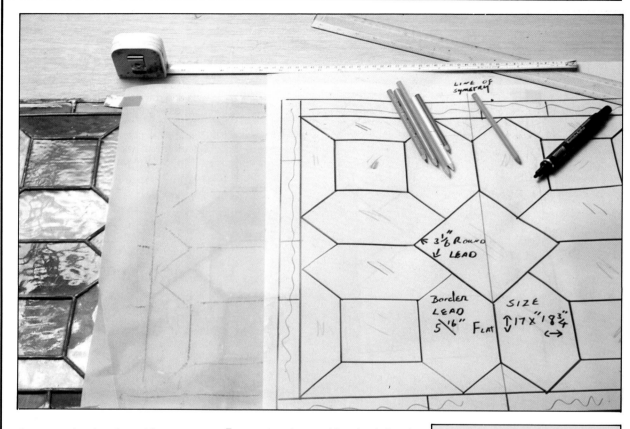

Annotate the drawing with comments about the color and texture of the glass and number the pieces in an orderly fashion to use as a reference when you are reassembling the panel. Mark on the new pattern the positioning of any copper ties for saddle bars or any other reinforcement. Matching the leads is a fairly straight forward operation. Measure the existing lead widths and check the profile to assess if they are round or flat. Measure the border-lead width and by using an equivalent width lead mark the cut line on the pattern. This is done by placing a short section of the chosen lead at each corner.

Ensure that the outside edge is lined up on the perimeter line by marking a dot on the pattern where the inside edge of the heart of the lead lies (i.e., where the outermost edge of the glass will lie) with a straight edge. Join up the two marks for each side. Place the window on a flat bench. Lay out the rubbed pattern alongside. This pattern will be used to place each piece down as it is removed from the lead. Keep the support packing in place in the case of a window that has bowed and will not lie flat under its own weight.

Before proceeding any further, run through the following checklist to make sure you have all the information: Size of panel — including template if necessary. A rubbing showing existing leadwork. A pattern taken from the rubbing, details of lead widths and positioning, glass colors, and textures. Suitable glass to match broken panes. Notes on the positioning of solder ties for saddle bars if applicable.

Holding the pliers perpendicular to the panel, grip one of the tails of the lead and roll it towards the solder joint, slowly increasing the pressure until the lead breaks free of the joint. Continue all the way along the first side. If any of the glass is free, pull it out carefully with your fingers.

Slide the window ½ inch (13mm) over the edge of the bench. Starting at the edge of the panel, grip the lead gently with a pair of pliers halfway between two solder joints.
Slowly pull the lead away from the glass forming a loop projecting from the edge of the panel. Make sure that you pull the lead along the plane of the glass; failure to do this may result in too much pressure being applied to the glass with the result of further damage. Continue this process all the way along the edge. Slide the work back onto the bench.

Cut each loop of the lead in the middle with a lead knife. Next slide the window back so that the edge of the glass is level with the edge of the bench.

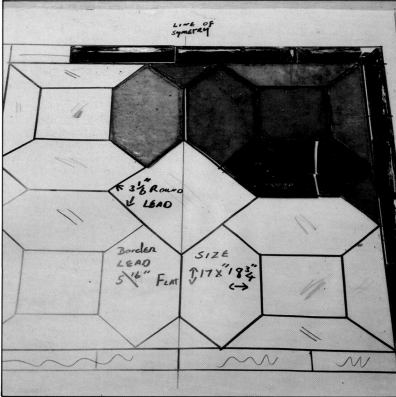

If the glass is cemented tightly into the lead the bond will have to be broken. Use the blade of the lead knife to gently scrape away the cement bit by bit. It is possible to open the channel of the lead to assist the removal of the glass but there is a very great risk of cracking the glass in the process. It is best to try to unlock a stubborn piece of glass by testing the pieces adjacent to it.

There is bound to be one or more that will slip out with less effort. With two or more sides free, the surrounding lead can be trimmed using the lead knife. Take your time and repeat this process across the entire panel. Lay out all the pieces of glass on the annotated pattern. Even pieces of glass that are broken or cracked should be laid in their appropriate position.

Once all the lead has been removed and the glass laid out, you can start cleaning the excess cement off the edges of the glass. This is done by carefully chiseling away the bulk with the lead knife. Before you start chiseling, select the side of glass that has the least cement adhering to the edge and place the glass this side up. When this side is cleaned, the glass is turned over. The glass should now

Start by selecting broken panes that are cracked but not missing any sections. Lay them on a sheet of paper fitting the pieces together to their original shape. Draw around the glass with a thin line. Use this as the pattern for cutting the new piece against. Cut on the inside of the line

Cut a clear glass template first to use during the leading process to check for a good fit. If it is suitable, then it is removed to be used as a pattern for cutting the correct glass. If it does not fit properly it is adjusted — either by nibbling away any excess or by re-cutting. If only fragments of glass remain in certain sections, keep them as reference for selecting glass and use the inked pattern to cut the clear glass template. Before any of the glass can be leaded together it must be checked against the pattern. This is done by laying the glass out

be lying flat on the bench evenly supported. You will have to exercise caution during the chiseling process to ensure the glass does not break. During this process keep the bench swept clean. Finally brush off the remainder of the cement with a brass-bristled brush. Spots of paint can be removed with a liquid paint stripper. Set all the cleaned glass in position on the pattern.

you have marked. If only part of the glass is present, draw around that on tracing paper and set this on top of the inked pattern. Line it up as best you can and continue with the remainder of the shape. This pattern will undoubtedly have slight discrepancies to the original.

carefully onto the rubbed pattern and making sure that it conforms to the line as closely as possible. Bear in mind that the rubbed pattern is not as accurate as a new pattern would be. Reassemble the panel as if it were a completely new piece of work. If each piece of glass is numbered before the panel is stripped down it will ensure that similar shapes will be replaced in the exact order they were found. **Refer to the chapter on tools and techniques for instructions for the leading process.**

It should fit perfectly; however, if the panel is too large or too small make a note of the discrepancy. In the case of the panel being too large, the perimeter lead can either be squashed or shaved to reduce its size. If the window is too small, extra lead can be added. Only as a last resort should the wooden frame be tampered with.

Once the panel has been completely reassembled then the rabbet on the frame has to be thoroughly cleaned of all putty and debris. Work with the hacking knife paying particular attention to the newly exposed face. It is essential that the new sheet of glass does not encounter any old putty as this might cause it to break. Ensure that no nails or projections are present. Lift up the restored panel so that the bottom sits on the lower rabbet and then lean the top half of the panel into position against the other rabbets.

Once the panel of glass fits snugly in position, it is removed and the rabbet is filled with putty. Knead the putty into a working-size ball, and start filling the rabbet from the top, by using the thumb to force the putty against the wood. Try to keep the amount of putty used fairly constant and keep your hands clean. If the putty is too sticky, excess oil can be removed by wrapping it in layers of newspaper and leaving it for five or ten minutes. If it is old and hard, it can be softened by mixing linseed oil with it. The putty is put in the rabbet before the glass to act both as a sealant and a cushion.

Once the securing nails are in position, then another bead of putty is applied to the perimeter of the glass panel and "faced off" at approximately 45 degrees with a putty knife. Start by placing the knife diagonally into a top corner and at 45 degrees to the glass. By keeping the tip of the blade in the same position, bring the handle in towards the top rabbet (e.g., in the direction of intended travel). This angle causes

Nails are placed in strategic places around the perimeter, one in each corner, one in the center, and if necessary elsewhere. Choose the positioning of the nails to coincide with points where internal leadwork meets the perimeter at a "T" joint. This way less stress is put on the glass. The nails used in lead glazing are flat headed tacks. They can be pushed through the outer lead, but

Once the rabbet is filled, the bottom edge of the glass can be positioned on the lower rabbet. The glass is then tilted forward at the top to meet the putty. Slowly work around the perimeter applying an even pressure supplied by the flat of both hands. It is best to start bedding the glass at the top two corners and work down both sides simultaneously, allowing the glass to slowly sink in towards the rabbet.

the putty to wedge into itself. Start moving along the rabbet keeping the knife at the same angle until you reach the opposite corner. With the other hand follow on behind and catch the excess putty. Do the top first, then the sides, leaving the bottom until last. When all internal puttying is finished, clean off any excess by cutting and scraping all in the same action. Finally clean the glass with a soft cloth and glass cleaner.

are more commonly laid diagonally across the top of the lead. Care must be taken to ensure the hammer does not slip off the head and crack the glass. Start the nail off by hitting it directly with a hammer and finish off with a suitable punch. If reinforcing bars are present, set them into the existing holes and tie them to the window.

Replacing pieces of glass will always leave the leadwork slightly scarred. It is therefore best performed on the outside of an external window. If the broken pane is on the perimeter of a panel, then the repair can be performed more easily by hacking out the putty or removing the beading to allow greater access. Finally if two adjacent panes are needing this treatment it makes opening the lead considerably more difficult as it is unsupported. If this is the case, the panel may have to be releaded. Assess the overall condition and if any other symptoms are present, perished lead, especially at the joints, other broken panes, sagging, and so on, then really the panel warrants a more thorough restoration.

When the cement has been removed, open the came by lifting the lead away from the glass. Lift the lead progressively further from the glass with several levering motions. Large leads are easier to bend than thinner leads as there is more room to maneuver. Continue the process until the flange is at least 90 degrees from the face of the glass.

Start on one side of the pane and work the leading knife under the flange of the came. Scrape away any cement you can, using the minimum amount of force necessary. Go over the same area several times to remove as much cement as possible.

Carefully break out the glass by crisscrossing the surface with a glass cutter. Avoid running the wheel over the same score line. Tap the scores from behind with the round end of the glass cutting tool. Remove the glass bit by bit.

With all the glass removed, ensure the channel of the came is completely cleaned of cement debris. Pay particular attention to the opposite leaf. This frequently retains a very thin layer of cement that must be removed to avoid breaking the new glass by extra pressure being put on it.

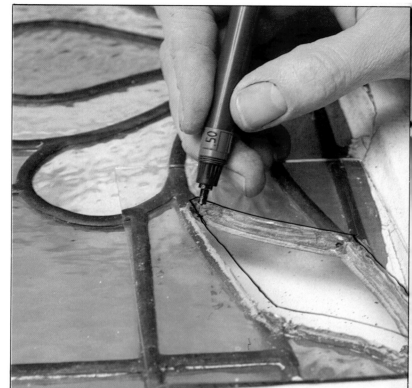

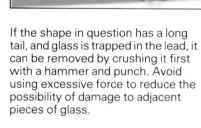

If the shape in question has a long tail, and glass is trapped in the lead, it can be removed by crushing it first with a hammer and punch. Avoid using excessive force to reduce the possibility of damage to adjacent pieces of glass.

The next step is to cut the glass to fit. Make a clear glass template first by taking a rubbing of the opening. Cut the template fractionally smaller than the actual opening to make fitting the replacement slightly easier.

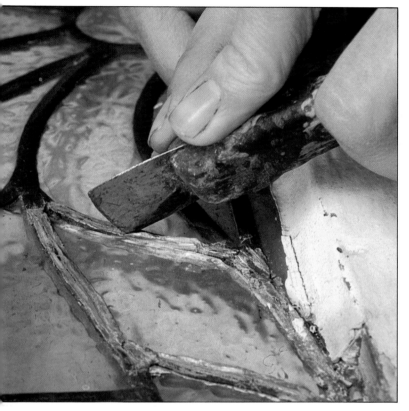

Check the template for fit, and make any adjustments necessary before you use it as a pattern to cut the actual piece to replace the damage. The glass replacement piece you have cut will no doubt be slightly smaller than the original piece of glass. Use a thin strip of lead as packing under the bottom of the glass if necessary, to keep it in position. Once the glass is set into position the flanges of the came must be folded back into position. Draw the blade of the lead knife along the length of the lead, repeating the process until the lead is flattened against the face of the glass. Support the glass from behind while you work. The corners and solder joints will never lie quite as flat as they did originally. To get the best result, continue to support the back side of the glass and lightly tap down the corners and joints with a hammer. Cement the gap between the flange of the lead and the surface of the glass. Mix up some putty and force it under the flange with a stiff brush. The cement should darken the lead and help to disguise any damage to the lead.

RENOVATION AND RESTORATION

Tape some tracing paper over the damaged area and make a rubbing of it taking note of the color and type of glass affected.

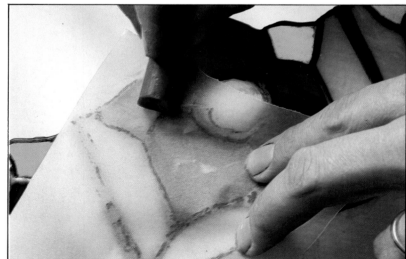

Score the broken glass and tap it with the rounded end of the glass cutter. Break out the glass from its framework making sure you remove all the broken bits. Some of the foil from the adjoining pieces may break away. They can be easily replaced and the affected edges will be covered by the new seam.

Cut and fit a new piece of matching glass, using a clear glass template. Refer to the instructions for copper foiling in the previous chapter where necessary. Lay the foiled piece of glass in position and build up the seam as you would for new construction. Make sure that the new piece of glass is properly supported while you work on the seam. You may need to coat the new seam with a patina agent to help blend in the repair. (See previous chapter.)

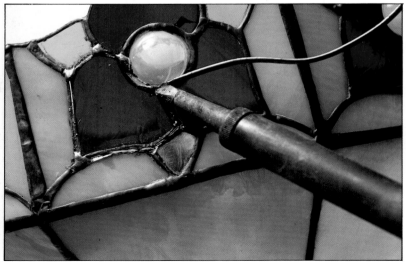

Using a hot soldering iron and a pair of long nosed pliers, move along the perimeter of the opening, and lift away the old copper foil and the excess solder.

Glass has an extraordinary charm. Once its power is laid over the artistic mind, an unending search will begin for ways of using this material. Glass is of considerable antiquity, and for millennia craftsmen have played with the medium, creating a plain and sensible window pane, or the convoluted shape of a perfume sprinkler.

Glass has been found on sites in Egypt and Babylon that date from 3000 BC. This very early glass was used to make objects, but after experiments in glass-blowing techniques, possibly in ancient Syria, the glaziers learned to make panes for windows. Glass was used in the windows of Roman Britain, and for centuries has been used to make an immense variety of things — jugs, vases, plates and bowls, lanterns, and candlesticks. But for a long period there were few developments in the decoration of flat glass.

The earliest example of cut pieces of glass bonded

together with lead dated from the ninth century and came from France. This exercise in leaded glass was a small panel that was destroyed during World War I. By the twelfth century, pictorial windows had become a major art form in Europe.

It was inevitable that if pieces of glass could be held together on a flat surface, the glaziers would realize that glass could be camed to form three-dimensional objects like lanterns or boxes. And other qualities of glass were realized too. For instance, it transmits heat very efficiently.

When Nathaniel Ward developed a glass container in which to grow plants, craftsmen found yet another model in which to play with glass.

Wardian Cases

These charming glass containers, used to decorate the home and delight any gardener of the exotic, were discovered quite by accident. Dr. Nathaniel Ward was a doctor based in London and he was also a naturalist. On a trip to the country in 1829, he found a chrysalis, the development of which he was determined to observe. He popped it, with some soil, into a tightly-screwed glass jar and carried it back to the city.

But seeds began to germinate in the soil, and even more exciting to the naturalist, they flourished in his airtight bottle for four years without the addition of water. It seems that the chrysalis was no longer of top priority to Dr. Ward, because he continued to experiment with plants growing in glass containers. In 1838, he made his first Wardian case from metal and glass.

These cases became very popular in Victorian homes, and a variety of designs were developed by the craftsmen, some of whom chose to design miniature copies of the Palm House at Kew Gardens, or the Crystal Palace. In deference to Dr. Ward, the naturalist, it should be mentioned

Below Glass alternated with empty space gives this planter a dimension of movement and shifting color.

that his glass cases were not used only to thrill home owners and keen gardeners. Other naturalists and botanists were delighted by the concept.

The Scottish botanist, Robert Fortune, in 1843 was employed by, and thereafter traveled extensively for, the London Botanical Society. He relied on Wardian cases to transport the plants he collected on his trips to the East. Using these cases, he took tea plants from China and introduced them to India's northwest provinces. And thanks to Dr. Ward's discovery of the principle of enclosed cultivation, bananas were cultivated outside China, and quinine-producing plants were transplanted from their natural habitat and grown extensively for medicinal purposes.

The Palm House at Home

Wardian cases, or terraria, create a self-contained world of soil, climate, humidity, and vegetation, based on a very simple principle. The plants absorb water from the soil, which then passes through the leaves and is given off into the atmosphere. The resulting moisture is trapped in the surrounding glass, where it condenses and trickles back into the soil. This process of recycling can continue for years in a terrarium. Dr. Ward managed to leave one case undisturbed for fifteen years, and he claimed the plants remained thriving and healthy without any care at all.

Tropical foliage plants and ferns are particularly well suited to this micro-climate of warm humidity. This is the feature that makes them so attractive for home use, for the leaves and textures of such plants are often beautifully colored and marked, and are very difficult to grow in more temperate northern climates. No wonder the Victorians, who so adored the decorative, loved these miniature glass houses. The combination of an ornate glass case, with rare

Left Darkened glass adds a quality of mystery and subtlety to the most ordinary plants.

Below left This planter resembles a terrarium but the plants must be treated as ordinary indoor plants.

and lovely foliage, is irresistible, almost a form of living sculpture.

The Wardian case allows an outlet for two forms of creative expression. A thoughtful choice of plants, mixing colors and shapes to form a little jungle, or a "minimalist" statement of one or two unusual ferns, can be an exciting process. Depending on the size of the terrarium, some landscape gardening can be arranged, with pebbles and driftwood. Or a desert scene with cacti may be preferred. The keen gardener can be truly creative at this intimate level.

The design of your terrarium will make new and interesting demands on your skill as a glass craftsman. The garden you plan must be included in your design. Try and visualize the combination of the leaf shapes you have chosen. Let your design repeat or enhance these shapes.

Because the plants must be clearly visible, the terrarium should be only lightly decorated with stained glass. A rhythmical motif round the edge of the container where it meets the lid is an obviously suitable solution. Corner bursts in colors that emphasize the colors of the vegetation can assume a strange interweaving with the plants. Perhaps an interesting color in vertical lines will allow for a mysterious glimpse of the jungle within.

The shape of your Wardian case can also present interesting design problems and should be connected again, to the style of garden you plan in this micro-climate. A landscape with driftwood and slopes would fit a simple rectangular design, but an intricate lace of delicate ferns may be improved by an octagonal lantern shape with a pointed lid. Perhaps you want to hang your terrarium near a window. The sunlight will contrive to bring sparkle and shadows, as it falls through the foliage and the sections of colored glass.

Right The delightful effects of light
and shadow are an integral part of
the pleasure in the terraria gardens.

Below This is an ingenious design
because the lid can be easily lifted for
plant care and gives ample space for
gardening.

It cannot be emphasized too often that the art of stained glass is also a craft, and it is imperative to make a detailed study of the effects you wish to create before embarking on this absorbing and demanding skill.

Design of Maintenance

Terraria rely on a tightly-closed, airless ecological system. The lid must fit very closely in order to maintain the system of enclosed cultivation. The only exception to this is the cultivation of a mini-desert with cacti growing in the sand. In this sort of garden, a small outlet is necessary, as these plants do not require as much moisture as a sealed case produces. The case must be thoroughly cleaned before any preparation for planting.

Lay a foundation base of small rocks, or gravel, to a depth of about 1 inch (2.5cm). This base can be made of charcoal as well. If your terrarium is fairly large, this base can be doubled in depth, i.e., 2 inches (5cm).

The soil is placed over this base. A good mixture will be made up of 1 part fibrous loam, 2 parts peat, and 1 part coarse sand; or another good soil mix is 2 parts of an ordinary potting soil and 1 part of extra peat. This soil mixture should be damp and is best at a depth of about 5 inches (12cm).

Do observe the moisture level of your terrarium. In a closed case there should always be a slight condensation on the inside of the glass. If this becomes very heavy, it is wise to remove the lid or open the door for a short time until the glass is dry. No condensation is cause for some alarm. Mist the leaves with a fine spray, and keep a careful eye on the state of condensation in case there is still a shortage of moisture.

Below Strangely shaped plants become even more exotic as they stretch past bands of frosted glass.

The Terrarium Garden

The basic drainage/soil base is prepared, and the exciting choice of plants has to be made. Your assortment must work visually, and plants of different heights will give an effect of space, or even distance.

One of the delights of a Wardian case is that it is possible, at this mini-level, to make a display of wild plants. On a walk in the country or on a picnic, make cuttings of such plants as partridge berries, violets, and ferns. Collect moss, and bark with lichen growing upon it. Even the seedlings of woodland conifer can be used in the terrarium. Carefully planted, with consideration to size and shape, and with the soft moss providing a ground cover and the lichened bark a textural contrast, your terrarium will re-create the quiet beauty of the natural woodlands. This does not mean that the real ecology should be disturbed in any significant way, and you should try to collect seeds or buy seedlings — rather than uprooting a growing plant. Autumn is the best time to collect wild plants.

It is wise to use small plants in a Wardian case, and they are best planted as rooted cuttings or seedlings. If your terrarium is fairly large, it is

Left The repetition of the arches in this classical style create a feeling of length and the reflection within the mirrors create depth. The terraria were designed to fit exactly on top of the tile pillars that are situated between the mirrors.

possible to leave the plant in its pot on the gravel/soil base. This is actually an ideal method of cultivating small orchids, such as miniature oncidiums or dwarf varieties such as *Dendrobium daggregatum*, or African violets. However most flowering plants are unsuitable for Wardian cases. The flowers rot off, and can spoil the balance of the cycle — in short, they are more trouble than they are worth.

Your nurseryman will be able to advise you on suitable plants for a terrarium, and he will also tell you to avoid rampant growers such as *trasdescantia*. However, here is a guide for you to follow:

Calathea oppenheimiana; Calathea ornata; Calathjea zebrina; coleus; Cryptanthus bivittatus; Cryptanthus tricolour;

Fittonia argyroneura; Fittonia verschaffeltii;

Maranta leuconeura Kerchoreana; Maranta Makoyana;

Neanthe bella:

Peperomia magnoliaefolia; Peperomia caperata; Peperomia sandersii and others;

Vriesia splendens.

Some easy plants with very pleasing leaf designs are palms, begonias, *dracaena*, and ivies. Baby's tears and ferns make good ground cover.

Closely sealed, and with a properly balanced cycle of condensation, the terrarium will make a lively ornamental addition to your decor, with a minimum amount of maintenance, only once every fifteen years if Dr. Ward is to be believed! It is advisable to scrutinize your little garden at least once a month — check the condensation, remove any plants that begin to rot and be sure to keep your Wardian case out of direct sunlight as the plants may be scorched through the heat penetrating the glass.

And, of course, you do not have to put a lid on it. Make a planter from rich, jewel-like colors and treat your begonias in the usual fashion.

Left Terraria make wonderful gifts for they complement any decor. Patterned leaves in this case echo their cheerful summer wallpaper.

Bright baubles

Louis Comfort Tiffany and John La Farge both adored opalescent glass. There is an exquisite Tiffany panel of cockatoos perched among brilliantly-colored leaves in the Haworth Gallery, Accrington in Lancashire, England. This glass mosaic is made from opalescent glass that has a thick milky quality such as is found in an opal and it was produced in a myriad of colors by both these glaziers. Opalescent glass is perfect when the shimmering effect of glass is required but the need for visibility is minimum, if required at all.

One of the most awe-inspiring examples of this application of glass mosaic is the "Dream Garden" designed by Louis Comfort Tiffany for the Curtis Publishing House in Philadelphia. The master himself describes this enormous work as "poetical and luminous idealism." Let us not be intimidated by the scale of Tiffany's genius as a glazier, but be glad that this glowing, cloudy glass was a result of his experiments. Let's use it in the best way we can.

It is a type of glass that may well suit the discreet designs of your terraria, offering a touch of luminous color in a thickened-cream design of

Above Plant shapes, the curves and colors of leaves, are thrown into new perspectives when surrounded by glass and barred by metal strips.

Below The comfortable chintz of this couch suits the clustered garden of the Wardian case. Placed within a well-lit corner, the plants will not be scorched by sunlight.

Mediterranean blue, leaf green, and intense gold, held up to a foliage of dense ferns.

It is certainly a type of glass suited to the making of baubles and sun catchers. Everyone needs, and loves, small boxes. Boxes to keep buttons in, to store earrings; boxes for paperclips and postage stamps, to keep jewelry, pencils, and all that foreign change from a trip abroad.

The enameled quality of opalescent glass creates boxes of jewel-like intensity. Small, mosaic pieces, held within an apparently erratic line of *cames*, are suitable for a hall table or a desk top, where the color effect adds a pleasant visual distraction from the more functional apparatus laid on these surfaces. A very plain square abstract in rich browns and golds might suit a more sober and masculine owner of the desk.

Little octagonal boxes, decorated with flowers and birds, are perfect in any bathroom or on a dressing table. No matter what the colors are, in such a small object, the eye focuses on only the glittering beauty, and its color scheme has no relevance to the wider color scheme of a room.

Stained glass boxes make excellent jewelry boxes. They can be made of a size to carry bangles and necklaces, and the design, intensely contrived in colors to match the contents, will create a beautiful, functional object that can be put on display, as a center piece on the dressing table.

Delight small children with a pencil box that has their initials or their name worked upon it, or a picture of their dog in mosaic on the surface. A little hanging basket of stained glass, planted with a falling ivy will become a treasured possession in the bedroom, the bathroom, or the kitchen. Just make sure you fit rings to loop a chain for hanging the basket.

Above These interior gardens, held and protected by glass, become novel and interesting because the effect of glass alters their usual appearance, as well as offering an extraordinary growing system.

CHAPTER 6

1

2

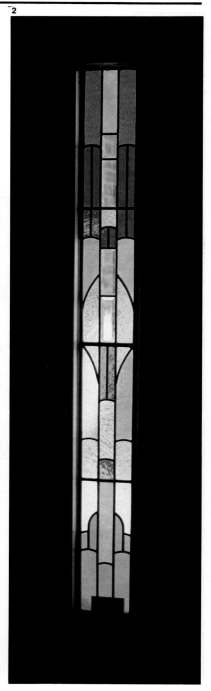

3

4

5

6

7

8

9

10

11

12

range of patterns for windows, lamps and terraria have been compiled in this chapter, for those readers wishing to construct their own stained glass creations. Alongside these patterns are details of all the materials necessary to complete the projects which are graded in order of difficulty—Grade 1 being simple, Grade 5 complex, and they range from simple light catchers to beautiful windows.

Grade 1 projects have been designed to provide a simple initiation to the practical side of stained glass and the complete process of cutting, leading/foiling, and soldering can be performed in a few hours, even if you are an absolute beginner.

Some cartoons have been reproduced to their actual size but in most cases this has not been possible. However, by following the simple instructions given in Chapter 3 — Tools, Techniques, Materials; you will find no difficulty in enlarging the design to whatever size you drequire. In fact, before you begin, it would be wise to study the chapter fully and carry out a few practice excercises on clear glass before embarking on any of these projects. This will increase your confidence in handling the tools and materials and minimize the risk of wasting some of your more expensive stained glass. However, should you experience difficulty in one or more of the processes, observe closely what it is you are doing and, most of all, have patience; the end result will be worth it.

There are a lot of stages involved in producing a stained glass window and, as with cutting glass, each stage becomes easier with practice.

Carry out each stage in the correct order and don't try cutting corners unless you are certain the result will save time without having a detrimental effect on the finished work.

Some stages are easier than others and some, such as soldering joints, may seem repetitive. Treat each action as different and observe closely the effects of what you are doing. You will find that soon you will be able to look back and see the whole process in perspective.

Before long you may wish to design your own projects, but bear in mind the catch phrase "Keep It Simple" and try to create, within the design, the simplest solution to the problem.

A selection of patterns for light catchers has been reproduced at actual size and can be traced straight from the book. These are all made using copper foil and can either be hung singly or, if several are strung together, as mobiles. These simple designs are a good introduction to the techniques of the craft but are also useful for using up scraps of glass left from more ambitious projects.

Safety First

Glass can be a dangerous material; always take care when working with it. By following the instructions given it is quite safe. However always keep a supply of adhesive bandages and antiseptic on hand. Lead and solder, if ingested, are poisonous, likewise are the fumes from solder. Avoid ingesting lead by regularly washing your hands, never eating, drinking, smoking, putting your fingers in your mouth while working, sucking the end of your pencil and so on. Also it is very important to clean and cover any cuts as lead can be absorbed in this way. When soldering, avoid inhaling the fumes by directing a fan onto the work. When cementing, wear a dust mask. The above precautions are no more than common sense; make them a habit.

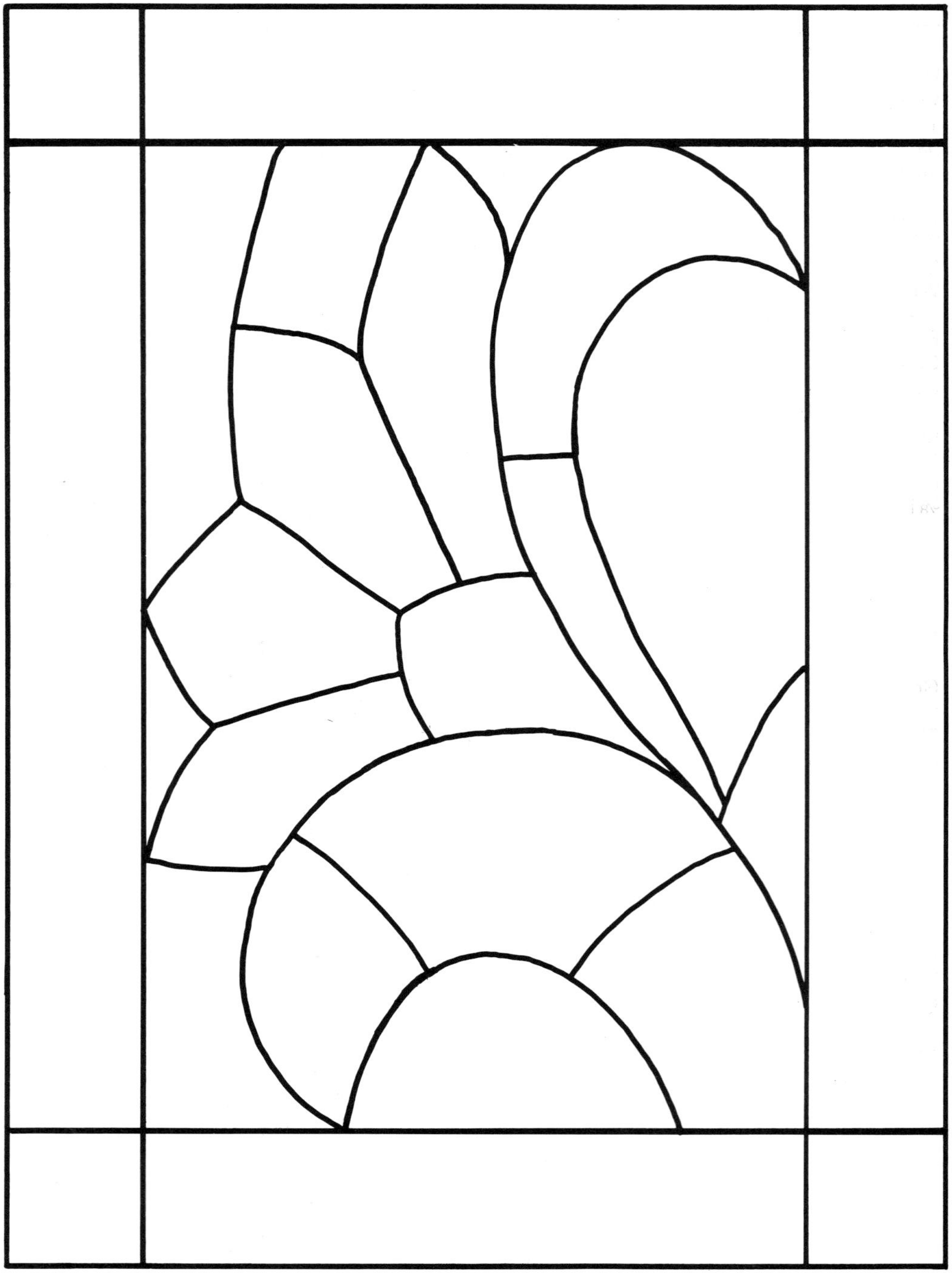

(9) Leaded panel

Grade 3
Composed of 31 pieces of glass
The following materials will make a
panel 18 inches (45cm) wide and 21
inches (53cm) deep.

Glass:
White	0.75 sq ft	(0.07 sq m)
Green	0.75 sq ft	(0.07 sq m)
White/pink		
opal	1 sq ft	(0.1 sq m)
Russet	0.25 sq ft	(0.025 sq m)
Gray/glue		
chip	1.5 sq ft	(0.14 sq m)

Lead:
½ inch (12mm) flat profile border
lead
⅜ inch (9mm) round profile
remainder

(10) Leaded door panel

Grade 4
Composed of 62 pieces of glass
The following materials will make a
panel 10 inches (25cm) wide and 30
inches (75cm) deep.

Glass:
3mm clear	2 sq ft	(0.2 sq m)
White		
glue chip	1.5 sq ft	(0.14 sq m)

Lead:
½ inch (12mm) flat profile border
lead
¼ inch (6mm) round profile
remainder

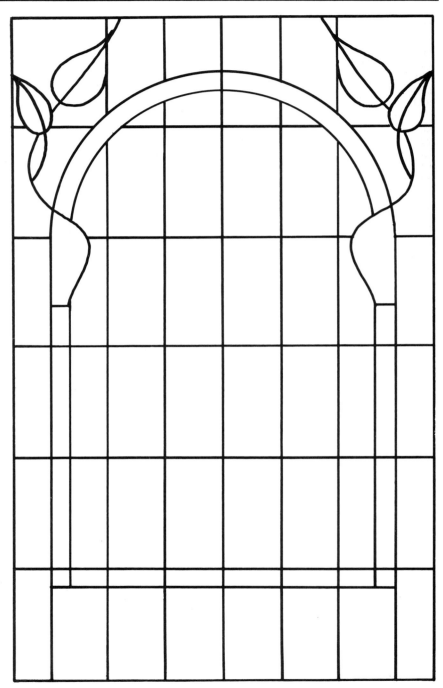

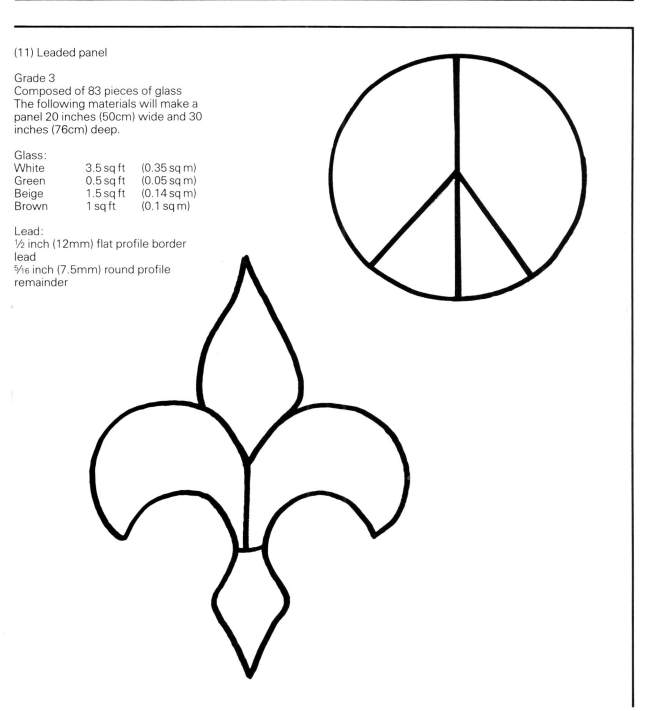

(11) Leaded panel

Grade 3
Composed of 83 pieces of glass
The following materials will make a
panel 20 inches (50cm) wide and 30
inches (76cm) deep.

Glass:
White	3.5 sq ft	(0.35 sq m)
Green	0.5 sq ft	(0.05 sq m)
Beige	1.5 sq ft	(0.14 sq m)
Brown	1 sq ft	(0.1 sq m)

Lead:
½ inch (12mm) flat profile border
lead
5/16 inch (7.5mm) round profile
remainder

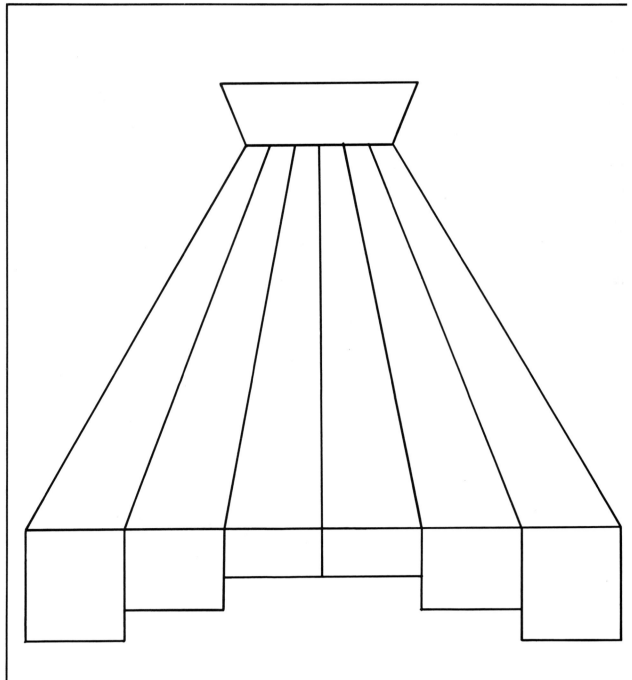

(12) Copper foil lamp

Grade 3
Composed of 52 pieces of glass
The following materials will make a
four-sided lamp shade 12 inches
(30cm) wide and 10 inches (25cm)
deep.

Glass:
Streaky opalescent
Amber

Other materials:
¼ inch (6mm) copper foil
12-15 sticks of solder
1 tin plate 3 inches (7.5cm) square to
trim and drill
1 bulb holder
Length of chain
Patina if required

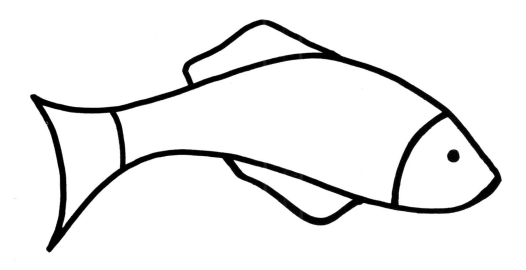

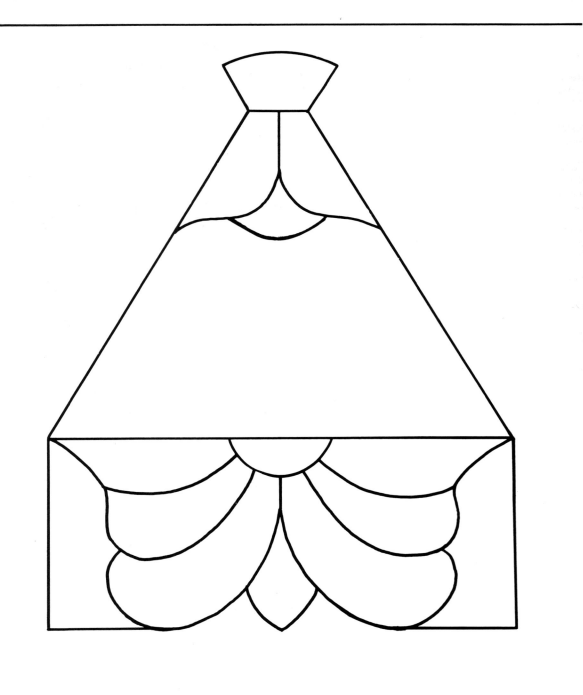

(5) Lamp shade

Grade 3
Composed of 60 pieces of glass
The following materials will make a
five-sided lamp shade 18 inches
(45cm) wide and 14 inches (35cm)
deep.

Glass:
All opalescent

Light amber 2 sq ft   (0.2 sq m)
Dark amber   1.5 sq ft   (0.14 sq m)
Flame   1 sq ft   (0.1 sq m)
Orange   0.25 sq ft   (0.025 sq m)
Coral   0.75 sq ft   (0.07 sq m)
Brown   0.5 sq ft   (0.05 sq m)

Other materials:
¼ inch (6mm) copper foil
12-15 sticks solder
1 tin plate 3 inches square (7.5cm
square) to trim and drill
1 bulb holder
1 hook and a length of chain
Patina if required

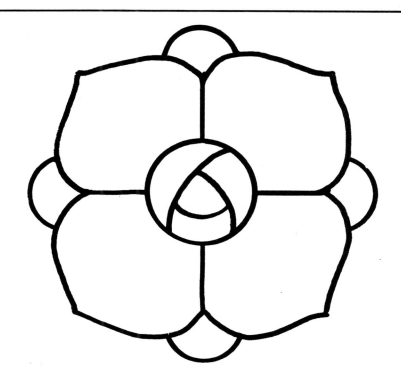

(3) Leaded window

Grade 5
Composed of 129 pieces of glass
The following materials will make a
window 22 inches (55cm) wide and
30 inches (76cm) deep.

Glass:
White	3 sq ft	(0.3 sq m)
Streaky blue	2.5 sq ft	(0.25 sq m)
Streaky mauve/blue	1 sq ft	(0.1 sq m)
Streaky pink	1 sq ft	(0.1 sq m)
Streaky green	0.5 sq ft	(0.05 sq m)
Streaky green/blue	0.5 sq ft	(0.05 sq m)

Lead:
½ inch (12mm) flat profile border
lead
¼ inch (6mm) round profile for the
main panel.

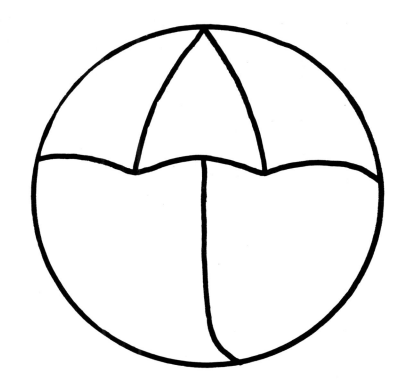

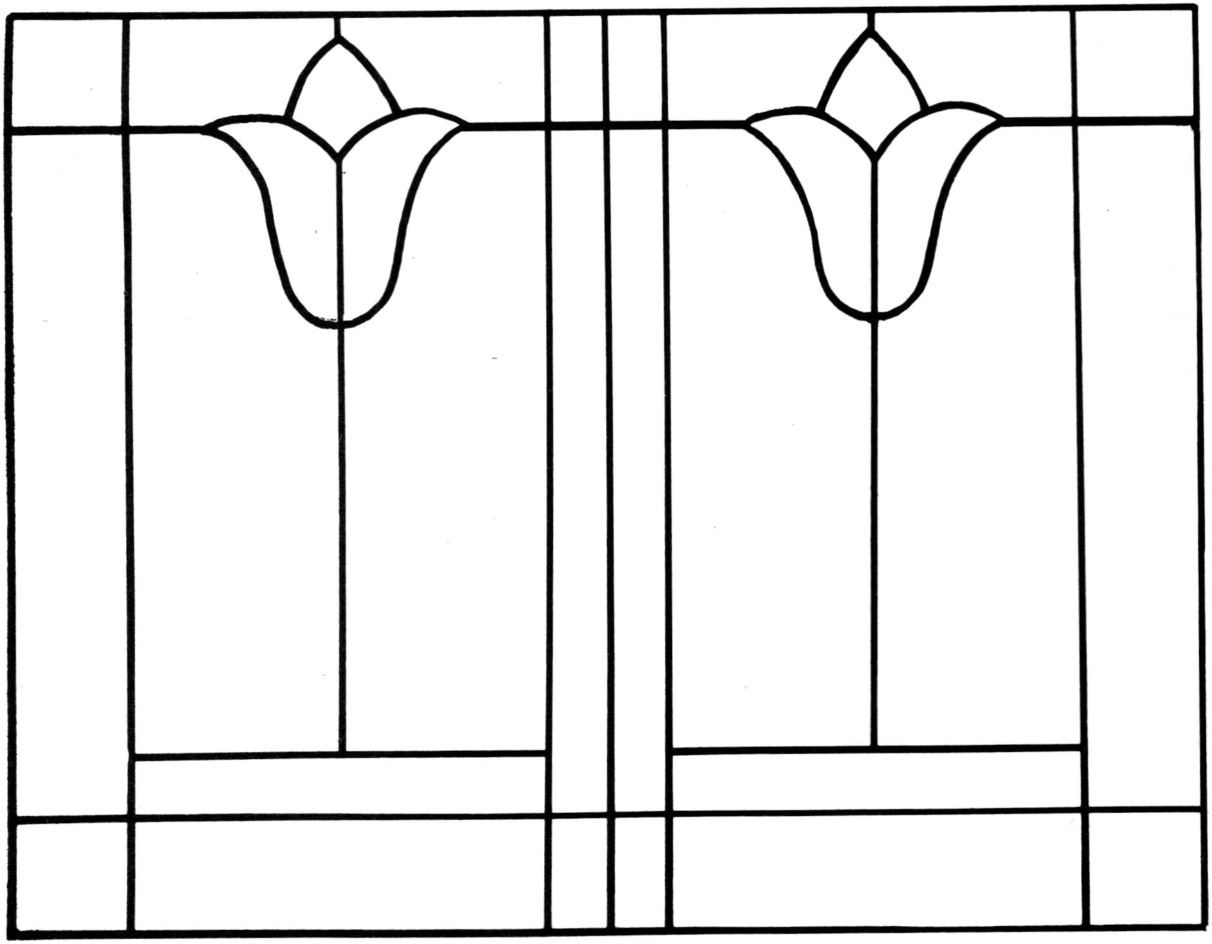

(4) Leaded panels

Grade 2
Composed of 30 pieces of glass
The following materials will make a
window 26 inches (66cm) wide and
20 inches (50cm) deep.

Glass:
White	2 sq ft	(0.2 sq m)
Dark green	0.25 sq ft	(0.025 sq m)
Light green	0.5 sq ft	(0.05 sq m)
Beige	2 sq ft	(0.2 sq m)
Ruby	0.5 sq ft	(0.05 sq m)

Lead:
½ inch flat profile border lead
¼ inch round profile for the
remainder

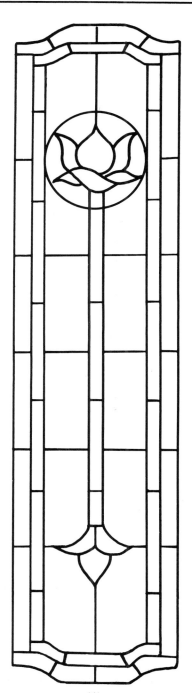

(6) Leaded window

Grade 3
Composed of 72 pieces of glass
The following materials will make a
window 9 inches (22cm) wide and 36
inches (90cm) deep.

Glass:
White	1.5 sq ft	(0.14 sq m)
Reeded	0.5 sq ft	(0.14 sq m)
Pink	0.5 sq ft	(0.14 sq m)
Light green	0.25 sq ft	(0.025 sq m)
Dark green	0.25 sq ft	(0.025 sq m)
Dark amber	0.25 sq ft	(0.025 sq m)
Ruby	0.25 sq ft	(0.025 sq m)

Lead:
½ inch (12mm) flat profile border
lead
¼ inch (6mm) round profile for the
remainder

(1) Leaded window

Grade 5
Composed of 201 pieces of glass
The following materials will make a
window 20 inches (49cm) wide and
30 inches (76cm) deep.

Glass:

White/clear	4 sq ft	(0.4 sq m)
Turquoise	1.5 sq ft	(0.14 sq m)
Beige	1 sq ft	(0.1 sq m)
Light green	1.5 sq ft	(0.14 sq m)
Dark green	1 sq ft	(0.1 sq m)
Light amber	.5 sq ft	(0.5 sq m)
Dark amber	.25 sq ft	(0.025 sq m)
Dark blue	1.5 sq ft	(0.14 sq m)
Ruby	1.5 sq ft	(0.14 sq m)

Lead:
½ inch (12mm) flat profile border
lead
¼ inch (6mm) round profile for the
remainder

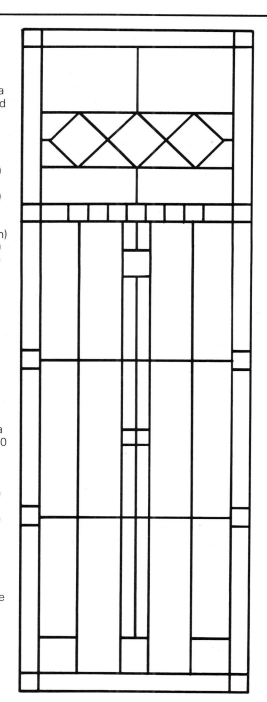

(7) Leaded panel

Grade 2
Composed of 71 pieces of glass
The following materials will make a
panel 22 inches (55cm) wide and 50
inches (127cm) deep.

Glass:

White	7 sq ft	(0.65 sq m)
Sand blasted	1 sq ft	(0.1 sq m)
Gray	1.5 sq ft	(0.14 sq m)

Eleven bevels

Lead:
½ inch (12mm) flat profile border
lead
⅝ inch (15mm) round profile for the
remainder

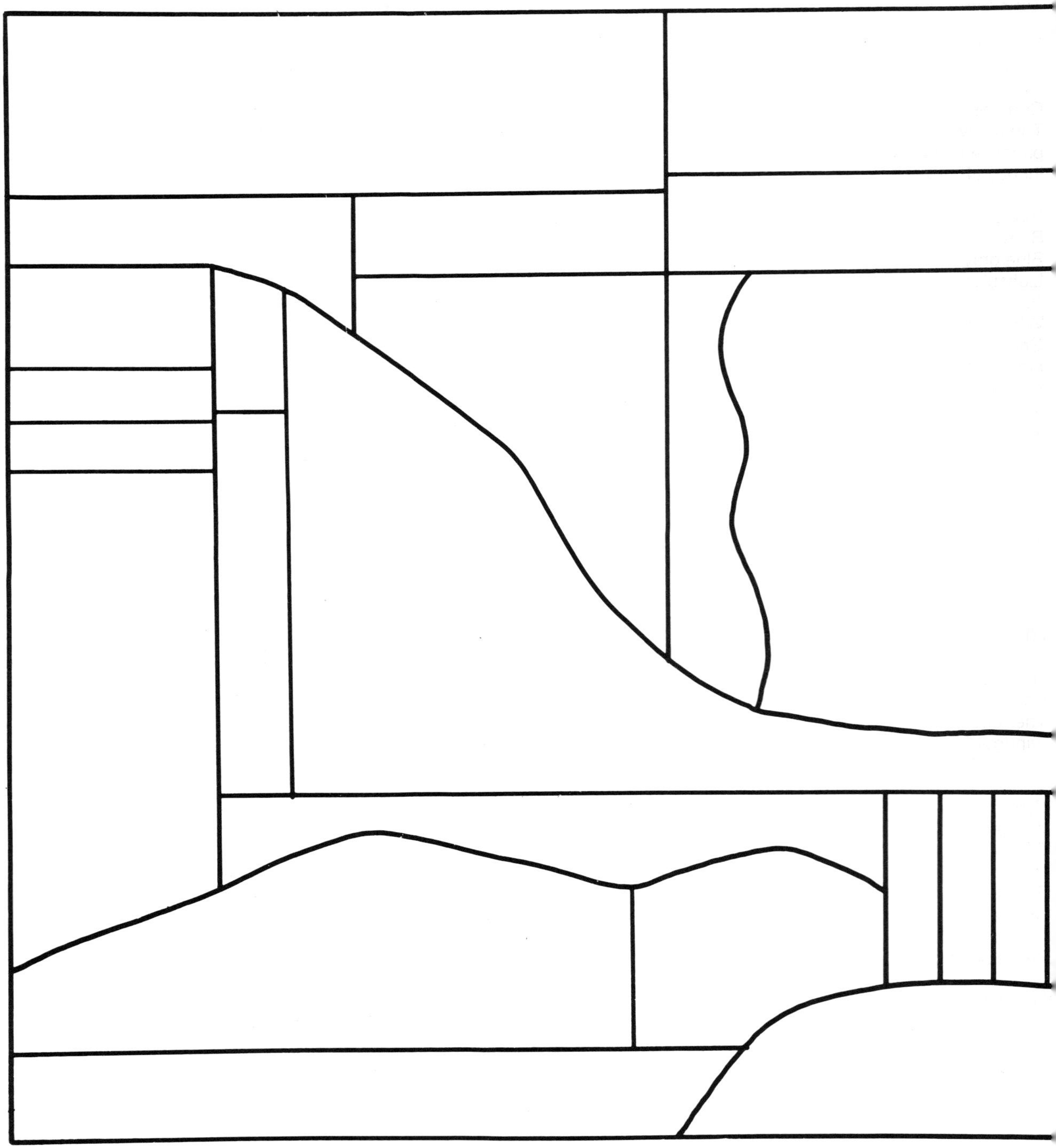

(8) Abstract leaded panel
A useful way to use off-cuts of glass

Composed of 25 pieces of glass
The following materials will make a
panel 14 inches (35cm) wide and 18
inches (45cm) deep.

Glass:
Ruby	0.25 sq ft	(0.025 sq m)
Blue/gray	0.5 sq ft	(0.05 sq m)
Light blue	0.25 sq ft	(0.025 sq m)
Gray	0.25 sq ft	(0.025 sq m)
White opal	0.25 sq ft	(0.025 sq m)
Green streaky	0.25 sq ft	(0.025 sq m)
Light amber	0.25 sq ft	(0.025 sq m)
Red brown/ streaky	0.25 sq ft	(0.25 sq m)
White semi-antique	0.25 sq ft	(0.025 sq m)
Pink	0.25 sq ft	(0.025 sq m)

Lead:
½ inch flat profile border
¼ inch round profile remainder

(2) Leaded Window

Grade 2
Composed of 38 pieces of glass
The following materials will make a
window 6 inches (15cm) wide and 60
inches (150cm) deep

Glass:
White/clear	2 sq ft	(0.2 sq m)
Gray	1 sq ft	(0.1 sq m)
Pink	1 sq ft	(0.1 sq m)
Brown	1 sq ft	(0.1 sq m)
Mauve	0.5 sq ft	(0.05 sq m)

Three bevels

Lead: 12mm
½ inch (12mm) flat border lead
⅜ inch (9mm) for the horizontal leads
¼ inch (6mm) for the remainder

Leaded Panel

Grade 3
Composed of 79 pieces of glass
The following materials will make a
panel 24 inches (60cm) wide and 36
inches (90cm) deep.

Glass:
Blue	2 sq ft	(0.2 sq m)
Beige	2.5 sq ft	(0.25 sq m)
White	4 sq ft	(0.4 sq m)

Lead:
½ inch (12mm) flat profile border
lead
⅜ inch (9mm) round profile
remainder except for
the circles that are ¼ inch (6mm)
round profile.

Leaded window

Grade 4
Composed of 130 pieces of glass
The following materials will make a
panel 20 inches (50cm) wide and 30
inches (76cm) deep.

Glass:
White
obscured   4 sq ft   (0.4 sq m)
Light amber   2 sq ft   (0.2 sq m)
Light green   1.5 sq ft   (0.14 sq m)
Light pink   1 sq ft   (0.1 sq m)
Light mauve   0.5 sq ft   (0.05 sq m)
Blue   0.5 sq ft   (0.05 sq m)
Orange   0.5 sq ft   (0.05 sq m)

Lead:
½ inch (12mm) flat profile border
lead
¼ inch (6mm) round profile
remainder

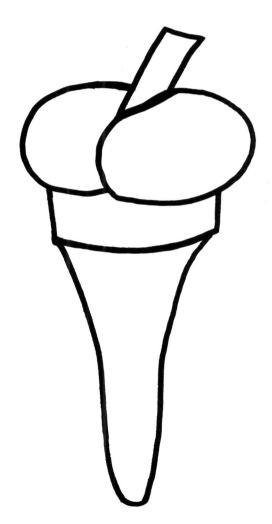

Landscape

Grade 5
The following materials will make a
panel 30 inches (76cm) wide and 42
inches (106cm) deep.

Glass:
Streaky green	1.5 sq ft	(0.14 sq m)
Streaky green/brown	1.5 sq ft	(0.14 sq m)
Streaky green/blue	0.5 sq ft	(0.05 sq m)
Streaky flame	0.5 sq ft	(0.05 sq m)
Light amber	2 sq ft	(0.2 sq m)
Dark amber	1 sq ft	(0.1 sq m)
Brown	1 sq ft	(0.1 sq m)
Blue	2 sq ft	(0.2 sq m)
Pink	0.5 sq ft	(0.05 sq m)
Mauve	0.5 sq ft	(0.05 sq m)

Antique glass Transparent glass, also called hand blown glass, which is produced by blowing the glass into cylindrical form. This is then cut and flattened out in a kiln. The blowing adds bubbles and other irregularities to the glass, which make for a more interesting transmission of light.

Bead Solder forms a bead when it is purposely raised over a solder line in copper foil work.

Bevel A thick piece of glass that has been ground and polished along the edges to give a central raised section. This allows light to be reflected in several directions at once.

Building board A piece of particle board larger than the size of the finished panel with two battens fixed at the required angle to conform with the outline and dimensions of the work.

Came This word comes from the old English word "calme" meaning string and is a strip of flexible lead, channeled either on one side or both, which is used to lead up pieces of glass arranged in a pattern.

Cartoon The drawing over which the stained glass is positioned during construction.

Cathedral glass A machine-made glass, transparent but nonreflective, needing a light source behind it to be appreciated. Particularly suitable for windows and light catchers.

Flux A substance, usually containing oleic acid or ammonium chloride, which is applied to surfaces to be joined by soldering to clean and free them from oxide.

Foil Thin strips of self-adhesive copper foil that comes in a roll and is used to surround the edges of the pieces of glass that are then soldered together. Most often used for lamp shades and other three-dimensional objects.

Glazing nails Also called horseshoe nails. Large nails with flattened sides that hold the pieces of glass and lead in place as the work progresses. If these are unobtainable 2 inch ovals are a useful substitute.

Grozing To neaten up by nibbling away irrregular bits of glass from the edge of a piece of glass. The notches on the glass cutter can be used for this but grozing pliers are more efficient.

Lathkin A tool used to open the flanges of the lead came to receive the glass and, in copper foil work, to flatten the foil against the glass.

Leading The joining together of pieces of glass using channeled lead, which are then soldered at the joints.

Machine-made or rolled glass This is produced by extruding molten glass between two rollers and often has a surface texture embossed on one side during the rolling process. There are two types, cathedral and opalescent.

Opalescent glass Commonly used in lamps, it is opaque, often of two or more colors and traps the light inside so that the glass appears to glow.

Patina A chemical substance (usually copper-colored or black) applied with a soft paint brush and used to darken lines of solder especially in copper foil work.

Putty Also called cement or glazing compound. A substance for filling the gap between the glass and lead thereby sealing and weatherproofing.

Solder A fusible alloy of lead and tin that has a low melting point used to join together the lead cames or copper foil when heated with a soldering iron.

Tie bars Also called support rods. Bars fixed horizontally across large panels of stained glass preferably along a line of pattern if possible, to strengthen the window and prevent sagging.

STUDIOS

ARIZONA
Robin's Stained Glass Studio
11424 N. 71st Street
Scottsdale, AZ 85254
602-998-3430

CALIFORNIA
Benson Design Studio
237-B N. Euclid Way
Anaheim, CA 92801
714-991-7760

John Bera Studios
774 N. Twin Oaks Valley Road
San Marcos, CA 92069
619-744-9282

Church Art Glass Studios
152 Helena Street
San Francisco, CA 94124
415-467-2869

Dave's Glass Art
1001 W. Foothill Blvd.
Azusa, CA 91702
818-334-0816

The Glass Works
300 Long Street
Nevada City, CA 95959
916-265-6700

The Judson Studios
200 So. Avenue 66
Los Angeles, CA 90042
213-255-0131

Nostalgic Glass Works, Inc.
1004 Brioso Drive
Costa Mesa, CA 92627
714-646-7474

COLORADO
The Boulder Stained Glass Studio
1920 Arapahoe Avenue
Boulder, CO 80302
303-449-9030

Creative Stained Glass Studio
85 S. Union, Unit C
Lakewood, CO 80228
303-232-1762

Simon Studio
28479 Douglas Park Road
P.O. Box 125
Evergreen, CO 80439
303-647-3489

Stowell Studio
600 Forest Drive
Bailey, CO 80421
303-838-5528

CONNECTICUT
Fredrica H. Fields Studio
561 Lake Avenue
Greenwich, CT 06830
203-869-5508

FLORIDA
Advent Glass Works, Inc.
P.O. Box 174
Fort White, FL 32038
904-454-3738

Casola Stained Glass Studio
11000 Metro Pkwy., Ste. 11
Fort Myers, FL 33912
813-939-0055

Glass Horizons, Inc.
333 1st Street, NE
St. Petersburg, FL 33701
813-823-8233

Conrad Pickel Studio, Inc.
7777 20th Street
Vero Beach, FL 32960
407-567-1710

White Stained Glass Studio
4242 Gypsy Street
Sarasota, FL 34233
813-923-4711

Woodbutcher's Stained Glass Studio, Inc.
1002 St. Michael St.
Tallahasse, FL 32301
904-224-3454

GEORGIA
Jennifer's Glass Works, Inc.
6767 Peach St. Ind. Blvd.
Norcross, GA 30092
800-241-3388

Seraphim Stained Glass Studios
464 Cherokee Ave., S.E.
Atlanta, GA 30312
404-588-1180

ILLINOIS
Botti Studio of Architectural Arts
919 Grove Street
Evanston, IL 60201
312-869-5933

Curran Art Glass Inc.
4520 Irving Park Road
Chicago, IL 60641
312-777-2444

Melotte-Morse Studios
213 1/2 South Sixth Street
Springfield, IL 62701
217-789-9523

INDIANA
City Glass Specialty, Inc.
2124 South Calhoun Street
Fort Wayne, IN 46804
219-744-3301

Fox Studios, Inc.
5901 N. College Avenue
Indianapolis, IN 46220
317-253-0135

Mominee Studios
5001 Lincoln Ave.
Evansville, IN 47715
812-473-1691

Moss Stained Glass
2501 E. 8th St.
Anderson, IN 46012
317-642-2788

Ragland Stained Glass
401 West Walnut
Kokomo, IN 46901
317-452-2438

LOUISIANA
Dittrich-Lips Art Glass & Mirror, Inc.
601 Phlox Avenue
Metairie, LA 70001
504-889-0631

MARYLAND
Art Glass Crafters, Inc.
16908 York Rd.
Hereford-Monkton, MD 21111
301-329-6005

Artisan Glass Works, Inc.
5700 Bellona Ave.
Baltimore, MD 21212
301-435-0300

Calligan Studios
8 Humbird St.
Ellerslie, MD 21529
301-724-3455

MASSACHUSETTS
Wilbur H. Burnham Studios
144 Turnpike St.
Rowley, MA 01969
617-948-3910

Cummings Studio
The Barn, 182 E. Main Street
North Adams, MA 01247
413-664-6578

The Lyn Hovey Studios, Inc.
266 Concord Ave.
Cambridge, MA 02138
617-492-6566

MINNESOTA
Gaytee Stained Glass, Inc.
2744 Lyndale Avenue S.
Minneapolis, MN 55408
612-872-4550

MISSOURI
Hopcroft Stained Glass Studio, Inc.
5810 Quincy
Kansas City, MO 64130
816-363-5810

NEW JERSEY
Hiemer & Company
403 Crooks Ave.
Clifton, NJ 07011
201-772-5081

NEW MEXICO
Art Tatkoski Studio
4801 Northridge Court, N.E.
Albuquerque, NM 87109
505-299-8113

NEW YORK
Chapman Stained Glass Studio, Inc.
212 Quail Street, Box 6032
Albany, NY 12206-0032
518-449-5552

Durhan Studios, Inc.
330 Eagle Avenue
West Hempstead, NY 11552
516-487-5656

Duval Studios
Gypsy Trail Road
Carmel, NY 10512
914-225-6077

Glass Artisan, Inc.
51 Brampton Lane
Great Neck, NY 11023
516-466-3890

The Greenland Studio, Inc.
147 W. 22nd Street
New York, NY 10011
212-255-2551

J & R Lamb Studios, Inc.
P.O. Box 291
Philmont, NY 12565
518-672-7267

Rambusch Decorating Co.
40 West 13th Street
New York, NY 10011
212-675-0400

Rohlf's Stained & Leaded Glass Studio, Inc.
783 S. Third Avenue
Mt. Vernon, NY 10550
914-699-4848

NORTH CAROLINA
A & H Art & Stained Glass
P.O. Box 35, Hwy 21
Harmony, NC 28634
704-546-2687

BL Stained Glass Design & Mfg.
124-A Wade Street,
Industrial Park
Jamestown, NC 27282
919-454-3196

High Point Glass & Decorative Co.
P.O. Box 101
High Point, NC 27261
919-884-8035

Laws Stained Glass Studios, Inc.
Route 4, Box 377
Statesville, NC 28677
704-876-3463

Stained Glass Associates
P.O. Box 1531
Raleigh, NC 27602
919-266-2493
919-833-7668

Statesville Stained Glass, Inc.
1103 Crawford Rd.
Statesville, NC 28677
704-872-5147

OHIO
Franklin Art Glass Studios, Inc.
222 E. Sycamore Street
Columbus, OH 43206
614-221-2972

Phillips Stained Glass Studio, Inc.
2310 Superior Avenue
Cleveland, OH 44114
216-696-0008

Poremba Stained Glass Studio, Inc.
20806 Aurora Road
Cleveland, OH 44146
216-662-8360

John W. Winterich & Assoc.
9545 (M) Midwest Avenue
Cleveland, OH 44125
216-662-2900

OKLAHOMA
Hendrix Church Art
907 N.W. 20th
Oklahoma City, OK 73106
405-524-2147

Tulsa Stained Glass Co.
7976 E. 41st Street
Tulsa, OK 74145
918-664-8604

PENNSYLVANIA
Edward J. Byrne Studio
541 Maple Ave.
Doylestown, PA 18901
215-548-2577

Hunt Stained Glass Studios
1756 W. Carson Street
Pittsburgh, PA 15219
412-391-1796

The Janross Studios
106-114 E. Main St.
Corry, PA 16407
814-838-1919

Keegan Stained Glass Studio
P.O. Box 297
Wycombe, PA 18980
215-598-7800

Pittsburgh Stained Glass Studio
Warden & McCartney Streets
Pittsburgh, PA 15220
412-921-2500

Stained Glass Specialists
910 Northern Blvd., Rte. 6 & 11
Chinchilla, PA 18410
717-587-4710

Willet Stained Glass Studios, Inc.
10 E. Moreland Avenue
Philadelphia, PA 19118
215-247-5721

SOUTH CAROLINA
Charles Towne Glass Studio
1079 E. Montague Ave.
North Charleston, SC 29406
803-554-9587

TENNESSEE
Emmanuel Stained Glass Studios
410 Maple Ave.
Nashville, TN 37210
615-255-5446

TEXAS
Harry Brown's Stained Glass Studio
910 San Francisco Street
San Antonio, TX 78201
512-734-2653

The Glass Gallery
P.O. Box 1042
Amarillo, TX 79105
806-374-7131

John Kebrle Stained Glass Studio, Inc.
2829 Bachman Drive
Dallas, TX 75220
214-357-5922

The Stained Glass Experience
1699 Junction Highway
Kerrville, TX 78028
512-895-4144

Texas Art Glass, Inc.
1211 Illinois St.
South Houston, TX 77587
713-944-2805

UTAH
Artistic Glass Co.
315 East 2100 South
Salt Lake City, UT 84115
801-484-8143

VIRGINIA
Lynchburg Stained Glass Co.
P.O. Box 4453
Lynchburg, VA 24502
804-525-6161

WASHINGTON
Mandarin Stained Glass Studio
8821 Bridgeport Way, SW
Tacoma, WA 98499
206-582-3355

Northwest Art Glass
904 Elliott Avenue W.
Seattle, WA 98119
800-232-3225

Perry Stained Glass Studio
470 Front St., N.
Issaquah, WA 98027
206-392-1600

WEST VIRGINIA
Shobe's Stained Glass Art Studio
1529 Fourth Avenue
Huntington, WV 25701
304-522-0308

WISCONSIN
Conrad Schmitt Studios
2405 S. 162nd Street
New Berlin, WI 53151
414-786-3030

Fantasy Glassworks
319 Appleton St.
Appleton, WI 54911
414-739-5762

CANADA
Artistic Glass Company
2112 Dundas Street West
Toronto, Ontario M6R 1W9
416-531-4881

Avanti Art & Glass Co. Ltd.
4956G-8th Avenue S.W.
Calgary, Alberta T3C0H4
604-941-8268

David Johnson Studio Inc.
1251 Scarth Street
Regina, Saskatchewan S4R2E6
306-359-3797

Design Glass Works
776 Corydon Avenue
Winnipeg, Manitoba R3M0W6
204-453-5208

Glassmith Studios Corporation
12730 127 Street
Edmonton, Alberta T5LLA5
403-454-6445

Luxfer Studios Ltd.
8481 Keele Street, Unit 6
Concord, Ontario L4K1Z7
416-669-4244

Savory Stained Glass Ltd.
210 Botsford Street
Moncton, New Brunswick E1C4X7
506-854-6062

ARIZONA
Lincoln Distributors
510 So. 52nd St., Suite 104
Tempe, AZ 85281
800-528-1419

CALIFORNIA
Franciscan Glass Company, Inc.
100 San Antonio Circle
Mountain View, CA 94040
800-227-8920

Glastar Corporation
20721 Marilla St.
Chatsworth, CA 91311
818-341-0301

H.C.H. Compounds
2109 Gaylord Street
Long Beach, CA 90813
213-436-4815

Hollander Glass, Inc.
10579 Dale
Stanton, CA 90680
714-761-5501

International Lead Co., Inc.
2700 Carrier Avenue
P.O. Box 911231
Commerce, CA 90091
213-721-4861

C & R Loo German Imports, Inc.
1085 Essex Ave.
Richmond, CA 94801
415-232-0276

ILLINOIS
Ed Hoy's Stained Glass
1620 Frontenac Road
Naperville, IL 60540
312-420-0890

INDIANA
Federal Bevel, Inc.
1111 Third Ave, SW
Carmel, IN 46032
317-844-8868

Kokomo Opalescent Glass Co.
1310 S. Market Street
P.O. Box 2265
Kokomo, IN 46902
317-457-8136

Thermoset Plastics, Inc.
5101 East 65th Street
Indianapolis, IN 46220
317-259-4161

NEW HAMPSHIRE
White Metal Rolling and Stamping Corp.
Route 12
North Walpole, NH 03609
603-445-5511

NEW JERSEY
S. A. Bendheim Co., Inc.
61 Willett Street
Passaic, NJ 07055
800-221-7379
201-471-1733

Canfield Sons
1000 Brighton Street
Union, NJ 07083
800-526-4496
201-688-5050

Reusche & Company
2-6 Lister Avenue
Newark, NJ 07105
201-589-2040

NEW YORK
J. Sussman, Inc.
109-10 80th St.
Jamaica, NY 11433
718-297-0228

OREGON
Bullseye Glass Company
3722 SE 21st Avenue
Portland, OR 97202
503-232-0776

WASHINGTON
Big M Stained Glass Co.
3201 4th Ave. S.
Seattle, WA 98134
800-426-8307
206-762-8005 WA

Fremont Antique Glass Co.
3614 2nd Avenue NW
Seattle, WA 98107
206-633-2253

Spectrum Glass Company, Inc.
P.O. Box 646
Woodinville, WA 98072
206-483-6699
800-426-3120

H.L. Worden Company
118 Main Street
P.O. Box 519
Granger, WA 98932
800-541-1103
509-854-1557

WEST VIRGINIA
Blenko Glass Co., Inc.
P.O. Box 67
Milton, WV 25541
304-743-9081

The Paul Wissmach Glass Co., Inc.
P.O. Box 228
Paden City, WV 26159
304-337-2253

CANADA
Classical Stained Glass Inc.
Hamilton, Ontario
416-547-3093

Desmarais & Robitaille Limited
Montreal, Quebec
514-845-2338

L.A. Stained Glass & Woodworking
Abbotsford, British Columbia
604-859-2079

Stevens Glassworks
Burleigh Falls, Ontario
705-654-4588

Thermal-Tec Industries Inc.
Winnipeg, Manitoba
204-663-3767

Toronto Stained Glass & Graphic Arts Inc.
Toronto, Ontario
416-763-6275

INDEX